APA and MLA Writing Formats

Revised Printing

Chalon E. Anderson
University of Central Oklahoma

Amy T. Carrell
University of Central Oklahoma

Jimmy L. Widdifield, Jr.
Contributing Author

PEARSON

Boston   New York   San Francisco
Mexico City   Montreal   Toronto   London   Madrid   Munich   Paris
Hong Kong   Singapore   Tokyo   Cape Town   Sydney

Dedication

To Sophie, Madeline, and Sylvia
—Amy Carrell

To the Anderson and Edwards families
—Chalon E. Anderson

To my mother, father, and sister
—Jimmy L. Widdifield, Jr.

ISBN 0-205-42437-6

Printed in the United States of America

10 9 8 7   08

CONTENTS

PREFACE

One component common to all educational endeavors is the ability to express ideas, research, and stories in a format that can be understood. Many students have come to realize that this means more than putting lines on a page. In the social sciences, a formal writing format is required. The writing format that has been accepted as the standard in the social sciences is from the American Psychological Association (APA). In English and many of the liberal arts, it is the format of the Modern Language Association (MLA) that is used.

Many students dread the inference and imposition of any writing format but understand eventually the need for consistency in formal writing. This workbook, which we have written to be "user friendly," is meant as a guide to assist students in their writing. The workbook is divided into three sections. Section 1 addresses APA and provides specific instructions on writing in this format. It also includes exercises to allow the reader to practice utilizing the various components of this writing style. Section 2 addresses MLA format. Section 3 provides a review of English grammar. This section also includes exercises to help the reader practice using the MLA. We believe that this workbook will also be useful to faculty instructing students in the use of these two formats, but we also believe that the workbook can stand-alone as a guide for students not enrolled in a research writing course. Finally, we have included manuscripts that have been formatted in both APA and MLA.

In any project such as this, there are individuals who provide invaluable assistance to the authors. We especially want to thank our contributing author, Jimmy Widdifield, Jr., a graduate student in the Department of Psychology at the University of Central Oklahoma. His dedication has been remarkable. He has served as a co-author and proofreader, and his computer skills helped pull this book together. We want to thank those individuals who have served as proofreaders for this book, Floyd Anderson, Andraya Anderson, Steven Anderson, and Suzanne Heflin.

Thanks also to Cherie Norvell of Allyn & Bacon for having the vision and foresight for this project and for her encouraging words. Also, we thank the Executive Editor at Allyn and Bacon, Carolyn Merrill for taking a chance on two novices.

Chalon E. Anderson, Ph.D.

Amy Carrell

On a personal note, the first time I saw any MLA style sheet, it appeared under my nose as I labored over a high school research paper. On the other end of that style sheet was my mother, Joyce Thomas, a high school English teacher with a penchant for precision. As I undertook this project, I thought often of her and the students she educated over almost three decades, including her own two daughters, in MLA style. If she were here, I would hope that she would approve of this workbook.

Invaluable help in the preparation of the MLA section of this workbook came from David Carrell, not only of Langston University but, as they say here in Oklahoma, "of the home"—from digging up sources to proofreading manuscript pages to buying and installing a new computer when mine gave out, his help has been without bounds.

Thanks also to Holly Easttom, now a graduate teaching assistant at the University of Central Oklahoma, for graciously parting with an undergraduate research paper for inclusion in this workbook.

Finally, thanks to my daughters, Sophie, Madeline, and Sylvia, for being patient.

Amy Carrell

American Psychological Association

(APA) Writing Format

The Basics: APA Rules

The APA has determined that manuscripts written using this format should follow specific

guidelines (American Psychological Association, 2001).

- The manuscript should be on white bond paper, 8 ½ by 11 inches. Pages should be printed on only one side of the paper.

- Standard margins are 1 inch on all four sides.

- The manuscript is double-spaced.

- Use 12-point Times New Roman or `Courier` font.

- The pages of the manuscript should appear in the following sequence: title page, abstract, text pages (introduction, methods, results, and discussion), references, appendixes, notes, tables, figure captions, and figures (the figures appear on separate pages, one per page).

- All pages are numbered, beginning with the title page, in the right upper corner, seven (7) spaces after the last word of the header, which is ½ inch from the top edge and one inch from the right edge of the paper.

- The Abstract starts the second page of the paper. The word `Abstract` is typed and centered one inch from the top of the page, on page 2.

- The abstract should not exceed 960 characters (approximately 120 words), including punctuation and spaces.

- The actual text of the manuscript begins on page 3. The title of the manuscript appears in sentence case, centered at the top of the page.

- Use words to spell out numbers one through nine and Arabic numerals to express numbers starting at 10 and continuing forward.

- When beginning a sentence, spell out the number regardless of the value.

- If two numbers are grouped for comparison, use Arabic numerals regardless of the numbers' values.

- Use Arabic numerals to express exact measurements.

- The primary headings (i.e., `Abstract`, `Introduction`, `Methods`, `Results`, and `Discussion`) should be continuous and should not purposely start a new page. EXCEPTION: Begin a new page for the references and appendix. The word `References` should be typed in sentence case and centered at the top of the page, as should the word `Appendix`.

- The first line of each reference is not indented. Each succeeding line is indented five (5) spaces, or ½ inch.

- The appendix follows the reference page. The word `Appendix` appears typed in sentence case, centered one inch from the page. If there is more than one appendix, use capital letters (beginning with "A") to identify each appendix. For example: `Appendix A`, `Appendix B`, and so on.

- If tables are included in the appendix, their titles must reflect the fact that they are part of the appendix (e.g., `Appendix Table A1`).

- If figures are to be added to the appendix, begin by identifying them by 1, 2, etc.

- All notes, such as author, copyright, and table notes, should begin on a separate page following the appendices. The title `Notes` is centered on the page in sentence case.

- All tables follow the appendices, and each table appears on a separate page.

- Tables and figures are numbered sequentially but separately; that is, there will be `Table 1` and `Figure 1`.

- All basic formatting rules apply to tables.

- When introducing a table or figure in the appendix, the words `Table` and `Figure`, with their numerical correspondence, are left justified and with the title underlined.

- The principle words in tables and figures are capitalized such as nouns, pronouns, verbs, and adjectives. Do not capitalize connecting words and prepositions.

WHY DOCUMENT?

When using the words or ideas of someone else, you must give credit to your source. If you fail to identify the source of the words or ideas of someone else, you are plagiarizing. Plagiarism is a form of theft—the plagiarist steals the words or ideas of someone else and claims them for his or her own. To avoid such theft, you have three options: direct quotation (see page 34), summary, or paraphrase.

PARAPHRASE

A paraphrase involves restating someone else's ideas in your own words, your own style, and your own sentence structure in approximately the same length as the material you are paraphrasing.

SUMMARY

A summary involves condensing someone else's ideas in your own words, style, and sentence structure.

SECTIONS OF THE APA MANUSCRIPT

A manuscript written in APA style should include the following sections in the following order: title page, abstract, introduction, method, results, discussion, references, notes, and appendix. The following is brief description of each section:

TITLE PAGE

The title page contains these elements in the following order:

1. Header and page numbers appear on every page. The page number appears in the upper right corner of the page.

2. Running head: An abbreviation of the title, of not more than 50 characters, typed in ALL CAPS. The running head is left justified and one inch from the top of the page (see section on Running heads and headers) and appears only on the title page.

The layout of the following components of the title page are centered:

3. Title of manuscript, typed in sentence case and centered. Double-space the title if it is two or more lines in length. The title should be aesthetically pleasing in that multiple title lines should be approximately equal in length.

4. Author(s) listed without professional titles and degrees such as "Dr., Ph.D." The affiliation(s) of the author(s) should also be included. Again, this information is centered.

5. If there are two authors from the same affiliation separate the names with and. If there are three or more names separate the name with a comma and use *and* to separate the last name

6. If the authors are from different instructions center the first author on one line and the affiliation directly below the line. Add additional lines for each author and their affliction.

Abstract

The abstract should start page two of the manuscript, with `Abstract` in sentence case (no italics, bold, or underlining) centered at the top. The actual abstract begins below the Abstract heading. The abstract of the manuscript should be a concise overview of the manuscript, containing the hypothesis/hypotheses and summaries of the method, results, and discussion sections of the manuscript. The abstract is typed in block form, meaning it is not indented, and should be equal to or less than 960 characters (roughly 120 words). All numbers included in the abstract should be in Arabic numerals; written numbers are used only to begin a sentence.

INTRODUCTION

The introduction section of the manuscript informs the reader of several items and usually begins with a general focus of the research or review being done and ends with a more specific, narrow focus. Early on, the introduction includes a review of literature pertinent to the focus of the current manuscript. The literature review should be concise and assist in fully developing a background for the focus of the current manuscript. Once this background has been established, the introduction should narrow in its focus and begin relating more to the purpose/focus of the current manuscript. Hypotheses should be clearly stated, and variables should be defined. Overall, the introduction section of the manuscript should set the stage for the reader. The introduction section does not receive a label. Instead, the title of the manuscript should be typed and centered at the top of the page, with the actual text beginning after it. The introduction section should start a new page. The methods, results, and discussion sections do not start new pages and should immediately follow from the previous section.

Method

The method section of the manuscript is a detailed account of the actual research being done and should allow anyone to replicate the research without difficulty. The method section is prefaced with the word `Method` (no bold, italics, or underlining) and is centered. The method section may contain any or all of the following subheadings in sentence case, and left justified: `Participants`, `Materials` (or `Apparatus`), and `Procedure`.

Participants

The participants subsection should include the sample size and pertinent demographic information (e.g. race, sex, age, etc.). Be sure to describe how the participants were recruited or selected for the research, including agreements and payments made. If using nonhuman subjects, include the genus and species or any specific identification information. Always include a statement reporting that treatment of the participants (whether human or nonhuman) in accordance with the ethical standards set forth by the APA.

Materials (or Apparatus)

The materials or apparatus subsection includes a brief but detailed description and explanation of the materials (or apparatuses, if any) used in the actual research.

Procedure

The purpose of the procedure section is to allow the reader to replicate the study, so the procedure

subsection should be a brief but concise step-by-step account of how the research was carried out.

All instructions should be summarized in a reasonable fashion. Begin by describing how

participants were selected, randomization, how variables were manipulated, and so forth.

Results

The results section is the component of the manuscript that provides a summary of the statistical

information, information on the research design, and the outcome of the data. The results section is

prefaced with the word Results (no bold, italics, or underlining) and is centered. The

following list includes all of the relevant information that should be reported in the results section:

- Summarize the main finding and results of the statistical data;

- In specific research designs (i.e., experimental studies, descriptive studies), be sure that the

  summary of the data supports the conclusions stated in the paper;

- Include all relevant results, but do not include individual scores from the dependant

  variable(s) unless, for example, it is associated with a case study;

- Indicate the significance or lack of significance regarding the hypothesis;

- Use tables and figures to add clarity to results;

- Refer to tables and figures in the text of the paper;

- Be very specific in the explanations associated with tables and figures;

- In the statistical presentation report, include

    1. Inferential statistics

    2. Value of the inferential test

    3. Degrees of freedom and probability

4. Direction of the effect

5. Descriptive data, including measures of variability

6. Justification of design and use of statistical test

7. All supportive information for parametric tests, randomized-block layouts, correlational analyses, and/or nonparametric analyses

8. Pertinent statistical power

9. Statistical significance

10. Effect size

Discussion

The discussion section is prefaced with the word Discussion (no bold, italics, or underlining) and is centered. The discussion section of the manuscript begins with a narrow focus and ends more broadly; that is to say that the discussion should begin by stating the findings of the research and whether the hypotheses are supported. Implications of the findings should be discussed in relation to the hypotheses as well as to previous studies done (those mentioned in the introduction section). Problems, or potential problems with the research should also be discussed. The discussion section should end with a more general discussion of the direction of future research concerning the research at hand.

References

The reference section of the manuscript begins on a new page. The word References (no bold, italics, or underling) should be centered at the top of the page. Entries in the reference list are alphabetized and should be typed as a hanging indent (the first line of the reference not indented and each succeeding line indented ½ inch or approximately five spaces).

Author Note

The author notes of the manuscript should start a new page and appear as `Author Notes`, centered at the top of the page. These notes have several functions. Most importantly, the author notes identify the author's (s') affiliation. Author notes also reveal sources of financial support, acknowledgment of professional contributions of colleagues, and provide contact information for further interest in the manuscript.

Appendix

Any appendixes to the manuscript follow the reference section. The word `Appendix` (no bold, italics, or underling) should be centered at the top of the page and is not followed by letters or numbers. Use letters only to discriminate between multiple appendixes, if any are present. Outline the materials presented in the appendix left-flushed under the appendix label. The appendix may include figure captions, figures, tables, printed materials used, computer printouts of data, and so forth. This first page is merely a list of what the appendix section contains.

ADDITIONAL APA FORMATING RULES

Running Head and Header

RUNNING HEAD

The running head of a manuscript is a summary of the title of the manuscript. The running head should not exceed 50 characters, including spaces between words. On the title page, the running head appears as `Running head:` and followed by the actual abbreviated title in ALL CAPS. The running head is located one inch from the top of page (standard margin).

Example:

Running head: ABBREVIATED TITLE OF ARTICLE

HEADER

The purpose of the header is to identify and organize the actual pages of the unpublished manuscript when the publisher's editors are reviewing it. The header is located ½ inch from the top of the page, followed by seven (7) spaces for the page number, and right justified. The easiest way to accomplish the page number within the header in most word-processing programs is to type the header left justified, space over 7 times, insert the page number, and finally right-justify the entire header.

Example:

HEADINGS FOR TABLES

Table headings identify the information presented in the table. Headings allow the reader to follow the data in an organized manner. Headings should be brief and identify the data below. APA format utilizes several levels of column headings:

- Level I: Column heads, typed just above the data covering one column
- Level II: Column spanners, cover two or more columns
- Level III: Decked heads, stacking of heading

Example: Level I

```
_____
Marriage
_____
```

Example: Level II

Marriages	Marriages
First	Second

Example: Level III

Marriage
First	Second

Running Head and Header—Exercise 1

Convert the following manuscript titles to a running head and header. Be sure to write each response following the appropriate formatting. For the header, use "1" for the page number.

Example:

The Effects of Color on Deductive Reasoning Skills in the
Classroom

Color and Deductive Reasoning	1

Running head: EFFECTS OF COLOR ON DEDUCTIVE REASONING

1. Sources of Stress and Interpersonal Support Among First-Year College Students

2. Role of an Abstract Order Schema in Conceptual Judgment

3. The Influence of Gender on Personality Development in Adolescence

4. A Study of the Conditioned Patellar Reflex

5. Attitudes Toward People with Disabilities and Judgment of Employment Potential

6. The Effects of Dominance Ranking on Sexual Selection Among House Crickets

7. A Study of Gestalt Therapy Techniques with Female Anorexics and Bulimics

8. Caffeine and Its Effects on the Central Nervous System

9. An Evolutionary Approach to Studying Mate Acquisition Among the

   Elderly Population

10.   A Review of the Book "Man's Search for Meaning"

1.
                                                                    1

Running head:

2.
                                                                    1

Running head:

3.
                                                                    1

Running head:

4.
                                                                    1

Running head:

5.
                                                                    1

Running head:

6.
                                                                    1

Running head:

7.
                                                                    1

Running head:

8.
                                                                    1

Running head:

9.

Running head:

10.

Running head:

FIGURES: GRAPHS & TABLES

When deciding whether to use a figure (charts, drawings, graphs, tables, etc.), always remember that figures should be used only to illustrate main points made within the manuscript. In this section, tables are columns and rows of numbers that report data, and figures primarily refer to graphs.

Here are the basic formatting rules utilized with figures:

- Figures must not "overshoot" the standard 1" margin.

- Figure titles should be brief and to the point.

- All figures must be referred to within the text of the manuscript.

- Be consistent!

When deciding to use a *table*, keep the following in mind:

- Tables are double-spaced, with a 12-point font.

- The length of the table should be ¾ the width. For example, if the width of the table is 4 inches, the length should be 3 inches.

- Each row and column should be labeled.

- Headings used for columns are centered at the top of the column.

- If the purpose of the first column of a table is to define variables, then that column is left justified. The following columns (those reported statistics) are to be right justified.

- Do not bold or italicize labels or numbers within the table.

ABBREVIATIONS FOR APA FORMAT

The primary reason for using abbreviations is to clarify and simplify writing. When deciding to abbreviate, consider the following:

1. Will the abbreviation reduce repetition?

2. Is there a standard abbreviation for the term?

3. Does the abbreviation lend itself to clarity and simplicity?

When choosing to abbreviate terms, remember that overusing abbreviations can confuse the reader and hinder comprehension. In addition, abbreviations used fewer than three times should be omitted from the manuscript, as they may be hard for the reader to remember. The purpose of utilizing abbreviations is to clarity and simplify.

The How's of Abbreviation

The term that is to be abbreviated must first be identified (spelled out) in the text followed by the abbreviation in parentheses. Once the term has been identified, it is then appropriate to use the abbreviation throughout the remainder of the manuscript without any further spelling-out of the term.

- NOTE: Abbreviations cannot start a sentence. Always spell out the term when beginning a sentence.

- *Figures and Tables*: Abbreviations used in figures must be identified in the legend or caption. Abbreviations used in tables must be identified in the title of the table or in a table note.

- There are some minor rules that apply to the use and place of the period (.) with abbreviations. Use a period with initials of names, abbreviation of United States, Latin abbreviations, and with reference abbreviations. However, do not use periods with state abbreviations, capital letter abbreviations, or with measurement abbreviations.

- When abbreviating the word *inch*, it is appropriate to use a period to avoid confusing the abbreviation with the preposition "in."

Forming the Plural:

To form the plural of an abbreviation, add "s" without an apostrophe.

- NOTE: Units of measurements are generally not pluralized. To make the abbreviation for page plural, however, use *pp*, not *pgs*.

Useful Latin Abbreviations:

```
cf.   compare           i.e. that is

e.g. for example        viz. namely

etc. and so forth       vs.  versus, against
```

Abbreviations—Exercise 2

Specific abbreviations are accepted in the APA form of writing. Below are some of the most common abbreviations. For the followings terms, write in the correct abbreviation in accordance with APA standards.

1. Intelligence Quotation   _____

2. Rapid Eye Movement   _____

3. Acquired Immunodeficiency

    Syndrome   _____

4. short-term memory   _____

5. Minnesota Multiphasic

    Personality Inventory   _____

6. for example   _____

7. and so forth   _____

8. that is   _____

9. namely   _____

10. versus, against   _____

11. and others   _____

12. centimeters   _____

13. seconds, minutes, hour (s)   _____

14. pounds   _____

15. degrees   _____

16. cycles per second   _____

17. decibel _____

18. degree Celsius _____

19. degrees per second _____

20. degree Fahrenheit _____

21. gravity _____

22. inch _____

23. kilometer _____

24. kilogram _____

25. kilometers per hour _____

26. liter _____

27. meter _____

28. milligram _____

29. million electron volts _____

30. milliliter _____

31. milligram _____

32. millimeter _____

33. miles per hour _____

34. Newton _____

35. pounds per square inch _____

36. revolutions per minute _____

37. volts _____

38. watt _____

39. kilohertz _____

40. volume _____

41. weight _____

42. gram _____

43. Hertz _____

Quotations

All material taken directly from any other document must be enclosed in quotation marks.   Keep in mind the following:

- Use double quotation marks when quoting material found in text; use single quotations marks if a quote is included in the original quoted material (see example 1).

- When referring to a document in the text of the manuscript, provide the author's name, date and page number(s) all in parentheses.

- Include the reference source on the reference page; all quoted material should be accurate.

- Cite references following the quotation

- It is the author's responsibility to decide if permission is needed to quote another person. Permission is not needed to quote from APA-copyrighted journals, as long as the quote does not exceed 500 words.

Example 1:

The last experiment that included freshmen in a

psychology class failed to support the hypotheses. Van

Buren responded to questions concerning this study by

saying, "sometimes this is expected in human research;

this is called ' cause and effect' and one can only predict

outcomes based on prior knowledge"

(Van Buren, 1977, p. 98).

- Include quotations up to 40 words in the text of the manuscript.

- When passage being quoted is longer than 40 words, create a block style paragraph:

    1. Start the quotation on a new line;

    2. Indent five (5) spaces (½ inch) from the left margin;

    3. Do not use quotation marks, type material within this blocked format;

    4. For paragraphs included in the block indent the paragraph 5 spaces from the margin of the quoted material;

    5. All materials are double-spaced.

Example 2:

Teall (1971) wrote,

> One of the most important men in the early exploration
> of Oklahoma never saw Oklahoma himself. The man was
> Estevanico – sometimes called Estevan or Stephen.
> Estevanico was a black man, and while much is known about the
> last years of his life and his death, little is known about
> his birth or his early years. (p.7)

- When omitting anything from quoted material, use three ellipsis points.

Example 3:

Carol's new car has a number of options, such as seat warmers,
special headlights, . . .all included in the 2001 model.

In the following passage insert quotation marks where appropriate.

The issues of aging and retirement are growing increasingly important in the United States. Advances in medicine and nutrition have increased longevity in our society and have prompted increased focus on the developmental life cycle of maturing individuals. Flowers indicated, the population would increase to thirty-four million by 2000. (Flowers, 1989, p.3) The "baby boomers" will increase the senior population by 2010 and they will make up the largest component of the U.S. population. Flowers (1990) further stated that, the 'baby boomer' will be the wealthiest group of seniors in U.S. history(p. 4). Other demographers agree with Flowers although they believe that her estimate may be a bit conservative. Only time will tell the actual impact of this population boom.

Anders (1990) has speculated as to the changes that we can expect:

As a result of this increase of older adults in the mainstream of society, it is becoming increasingly more important that theorist and researchers understand many of the complex psychological and social issues relative to this expanding group of our society. Among other things, 'retirees' are likely to feel stress and anxiety in dealing with the role transitions, the prospect of isolation and loneliness, the possible loss of societal role and status, financial instability, and the inevitable decline in health and loss of independence. (p. 4).

Anders (1991) introduces the issue of the retirement role that the 'boomer' will assume. Retirement became a tangible life event in 1935 with the enactment of Social Security legislation. The law provided individuals with a financial supplement in old age and thus established retirement as a social institution (p.7).

REFERENCING IN APA FORMAT

Basic rules of referencing:

1. Do not indent the first line of a reference; the first line of a reference will be one inch from the left margin (a hanging indention). Indent the succeeding lines ½ inch (5 spaces).

2. All references are double-spaced, with no additional line spaces between references.

3. References are alphabetized according the first author's last name. Use the following author's last name to continue alphabetizing only if the first author's name is listed more than once. If no author is listed, alphabetized according to the title of whatever is being referenced.

4. Use periods after each letter of the author's first and middle initials.

5. Space one time after each period in the reference to conserve space.

PERIODICALS:

Last Name, Initial(s) (Year/Date of Publication). Title of article is listed here. *Name of Journal, volume number*(issue number), page numbers.

Last Name, Initial(s): List all authors of the publication in the order they are listed on the actual publication. Spell out the last name(s) and follow with the first initial (and middle initial if given) and a period. In the case of multiple authors, list all authors using the ampersand symbol (&) to separate the next to last and/or last author's names.

The format for authorship is the same for all referencing. The exception to this format is authorship without specific individuals, such as no author.

(Year/Date of Publication): Type the year in parentheses. Occasionally, a month or season, depending on the publication, will be given. In the latter case, type the year first followed by a comma and then the month or season.

Title: Type the full title of the article. Capitalize only the first letter of the first word of the title and any proper nouns. If there is a subtitle, conclude the title with a colon (:), and capitalize the first letter of the first word of the subtitle.

Name of Journal: *Italicize* the full name of the journal from which the article appeared. Follow the name of the journal with a comma.

Volume Number and Issue Number: *Italicize* the volume number of the journal. If the journal citation does not list an issue number, follow the volume number with a comma. In the case that an issue number is listed, follow the volume number with no punctuation and instead with the issue number in parentheses, *not italicized*, followed by a comma.

Page Numbers: Type the page number(s) separated by a dash (-), concluding with a period.

```
Burris, K., & Berry, Z. (1980). The life and times of Mary.
     Evolution, 61(9), 491-499.
```

Magazines: Referencing magazines are similar to periodicals with only one difference. When typing the Year/Date of Publication, include the year, month, and date (if given).

Conn, B. N., & Conn, H. L. (1992, June 26). The effects of

    caffeine on spatial patterning. *Physiological Psychology, 3*

    (2), 26 - 39.

5

<u>Newsletter article</u>: Referencing an article from a newsletter follows the same format as a general periodical.

Schmidt, I. M. (1987, Fall). Parenting styles applied to today's

    generation. *Parenting Psychology, 13*, 3 - 6.

<u>Daily/weekly newspaper article</u>: Referencing newspaper articles are similar to magazines with only one difference. Page numbers are preceded by p. or pp. If pages numbers are discontinuous, list all page numbers, separating the page numbers with commas.

Brixey, J. (2000, May 5). Environmental factors in biology shed

    light on insurance claims. *The Houston Weekly,* p. C4.

BOOKS:

Last Name, Initial(s). (Year of Publication). *Title of book goes*

    here (Edition). Location of Publisher: Name of Publisher.

Year of Publication: List the year that the book was published.

Edition: If the book includes an edition, which is usually a number, enclose it in parentheses immediately following the title of the book. Use the abbreviation of "ed." when listing the number of edition. Do not italicize the information regarding the edition.

Location of Publisher: Type the city and state (or country if outside the United States), followed by a colon (:). The exception to listing city and state is when the city is well known (e.g., San Francisco, New York, London, etc...)

Name of Publisher: Identify the publishing company that published the book, followed by a period.

```
Mitchell, J. (1982). The mythos of homosexuality (2ed.). London:
    Express Publishers.
```

Article or chapter in an edited book

```
Last Name, Initial(s). (Year of Publication). Title of article or
    book chapter goes here. In Initials., Last Name (Eds.), Title
    of book (page numbers). Location of Publisher: Name of
    Publisher.
```

IN Initials., Last Name: The names of the book's editor(s) are listed reversed, the first and middle initials precede the last name.

Page numbers: preface the page numbers with *pp.*, or *p.* if only one page.

Bond, V. (1980). The psychology of life: Working with blended

    families. IN J. Wynn, Jr., M. White, & M. Boat (Eds.). *Family*

    Psychology (pp. 27-36). Boston, MA: Brooks.

In case no author or editor is listed, alphabetize (excluding a, an, *and* the*) the entry according to*

the first word in the title of the book.

When referencing the Diagnostic and Statistical Manual of Mental Disorders, use the following

basic citation reference, filling in the necessary information:

American Psychiatric Association. (19xx). *Diagnostic and*

    statistical manual of mental disorders (xx ed.). Washington,

    DC: Author.

Publication Information:

DSM–III – R	(1987)	3rd ed., revised
DSM–IV	(1994)	4th ed.
DSM–IV–TR	(2000)	text revision

BROCHURES:

Last Name, Initial(s). (Year of Publication). *Title of brochure.*

    [Brochure]. Location of Publisher: Name of Publisher.

Reference a brochure as if it were a book. Note that the [Brochure] is typed in brackets following

the edition.

Christie, A., Capp, W., & Goyle, C. J. (1976). *A basic approach to*

        cardiovascular disease [Brochure]. St. Louis: Mandalay.

DISSERTATIONS & THESES ABSTRACTS

Dissertations and Masters theses are referenced in the same format:

Published Doctoral or Masters Dissertation:

Last Name, Initial(s). (Year of Publication). Title of

        dissertation. *Dissertation/Masters Abstracts International,*

        volume number (issue number if given), page number.

In case that the dissertation is retrieved from microfilm, follow the page number with the following

information contained in pararentheses: University Microfilms No. XXXXX-XXXXX. End the

citation with a period.

Eden, D. K. (1971). Cost accounting: The necessary core in

        accounting. *Dissertations Abstracts International, 35*

        (X51007), 1981E.

Unpublished Doctoral or Masters Dissertation:

Last Name, Initial(s). (Year Written). *Title of dissertation.*

        Unpublished doctoral/masters dissertation, Name of

        University, City of University, State.

Cumby, D. (1985). *Dentistry and the stress placed on children.*
Unpublished doctoral dissertation, University of California,
Davis.

REVIEWS OF BOOKS, FILMS, & VIDEOS:

Last Name, First Initial. (Year of Publication). Title of review
[Review of the book/film/video *Title of book/film/video*].
Name of Journal, Volume Number, issue number, page numbers.

Title of Review: If a title is not given for the actual review, use the information inside the brackets
as the title.

Ravencroft, A. (2001). NRMs in children's cartoons [Review of the
film *The witch of riverbend*]. *Journal of Children's Media, 1,*
4-6.

UNPUBLISHED PAPER PRESENTED AT A MEETING:

Last Name, First Initial. (Year of Meeting, Month). *Title of
Unpublished paper.* Paper presented at the meeting of Title of
Meeting, City, State.

Title of Meeting: Insert the title of the meeting.

Harris, D. (2001, May). *Stress and daily hassles.* Paper presented
at the meeting of the Association for International Medicine,
Chicago, IL.

POSTER SESSION:

Last Name, Initial(s). (Year of session, Month). *Title of Poster.*

    Poster session presented at the annual meeting of the Name of

    Organization Sponsoring Session, City, State.

Name of Organization Sponsoring Session: Insert the name of the organization that is sponsoring

the poster session. The title of the poster should be in italics.

Tate, E. (1999, September). *Diversity in the U.S.* Poster

    session presented at the regional meeting of the

    Multicultural Society of America, Denver, CO.

UNPUBLISHED MANUSCRIPT NOT SUBMITTED FOR PUBLICATION:

Last Name, Initial(s). (Year Manuscript was written). *Title of*

    unpublished manuscript. Unpublished manuscript.

Brixey, D., & Smart, J. (1994). *Seniors adults: Pedagogical*

    strategies for teaching computer technology. Unpublished

    manuscript.

ELECTRONIC MEDIA:

On-line Journal:

Last Name, Initial(s). (Year of Publication). Title of article.

    Name of periodical. Retrieved Month day, Year, from

    http://specify path here

Specify path here: insert the web address from which the article came. If the article is retrieved via file transfer protocol (ftp), replace `http` with `ftp`.

```
Mayfield, A. R. (1991). Computer data on-line. Computers Today.

    Retrieved August 29, 1999, http://www.comptoday.com
```

On-line Newsletter: Referencing an on-line newsletter follows the same format as an on-line article.

```
McDermott, P. S. (1999, October). The use of meditation for simple

    phobias. Empirical News. Retrieved April 19, 2001, from

    http://www.emipiricalnews.net
```

Abstract on CD-ROM:

```
Last Name, Initial(s). (Year of Publication). Title of article.

    [CD-ROM]. Title of Journal, Volume Number, issue number.

    Abstract from: Source and Retrieval Number.
```

```
Thomas, D. C., & Chalon, A. E. (1954). Will computers become a

    tool in the future. [CD-ROM]. Business Chronicle, 63. Abstract

    from: Business File: Abstract Item: R19510.
```

- *Always provide enough information in on-line referencing so that repeated retrieval is possible.*

- *Specify the specific source of the material i.e., web cite, email, abstract, CD-Rom and database.*

Television Broadcast:

Last Name, Initial(s). (Position of author). (Year, Month, Day of Broadcast). *Title of Television Program*. [Television broadcast]. City, State of Distributor: Name of Broadcasting Company.

Position of author: Place the official title of the author, writer, producer, etc. in parentheses (i.e., producer, director, etc.) after the name.

Murray. S. (Executive Producer). (1999, November 2). *60 Minutes* [Television broadcast]. New York: Columbia Broadcasting.

Television Series

Last Name, Initial(s). (Producer). (Year of Broadcast). *Title of television series* [Television series]. City, State of Distributor: Name of Broadcasting Company.

Alphabetize the entry by the last name of the producer.

Baily, L. (Producer). (1997) *City in focus* [Television series]. Los Angeles: American Broadcasting Company.

Referencing—Exercise 4

Correct the following incorrect reference citations.

1. Bowen, R. (1954). The Joy of Writing. *People* March. Page 47-
   49.

   _____

   _____

   _____

2. Toby, E., Maxwell, C. & Carpenter, Q. (2000). A guide to
   marriage. Family Issues, 30, 401-413.

   _____

   _____

   _____

3. Butler, Wes., Cooper, J., Bold, R. & White, B. (1996). *The
   Tie that Binds: A new edition.* New York: Bacon Publishers.

   _____

   _____

   _____

4. Mason, Tom, Dr.(1887). Returning to the Midwest. In K.

   Wright & B. Wright (Eds.),Insight on the cities in the

   Midwest. (pp. 104-109. Kansas City: Hill.

   _____

   _____

   _____

5. Boss, A. Y. (1997). An examination of adult behavior: When

   stress is controlled (Doctoral dissertation, University of

   Maryland, 1997). Dissertation Abstracts International, 31,

   W80176.

   _____

   _____

   _____

6. Wilson, C. (1995). Spanish as a second language. Unpublished

   master's thesis, Austin Texas, University of Texas

   _____

   _____

   _____

7. Zane, G. E. & Falcon, B. (1988). The Development of a

   Politician (Review of the book *Politicians and Why*). Los

   Angeles: Fox Publishers.

---

8. Eaton, W., Scott, R., Clarke, U., and O, Lyons, (1978). A

   New Approach to Teaching Using Technology. <u>Technology Today,</u>

   <u>9,</u> 90-97.

Referencing—Exercise 5

The following references include periodicals, books, theses, reviews, and materials in press.

Correct the following citations.

1. Green, Von & Kate Ball (1991). Understanding Behavior 101. Psychology In the Twenty-First Century. Vol. 8, page 312-324.

   _____

   _____

   _____

2. Stanley, T. Y., Ross, E., Franklin, D. A. and Boyd, G. H. (in press). Relationships: A new beginning. <u>Directions, 6,</u> pp. 89-95.

   _____

   _____

   _____

3. Hightower, Y. and Cobb, M. (Eds.). (1978). *Senior Adulthood in Different Cultures*. Macmillan: Philadelphia.

   _____

   _____

   _____

4. Timberland, S. (1967). Life began at 40. M. Hart (Ed.),
   Developmental Issues for Men and Women. (pp. 1234-1240).
   Kansas City: Dell.

_____

_____

_____

5. Baxter R., Young, L. & Grayson, O.P, (1988, January). Family
   histories using color genograms. Paper session presented at
   the biannual meeting of the American Society of Medicine,
   Alexander, SC.

_____

_____

_____

6. The approach to examining child in dysfunctional families.
   (1989). Jordan, Z. Unpublished manuscript.

_____

_____

_____

7. Simpson, W. (1998). The code of silence in Greek lettered

organizations. (Review of film). Student service series. Vol.

6.

_____

_____

_____

Referencing—Exercise 6

From the following information create the appropriate reference.

1. **Author(s) Name(s)**   Carol Biggs, Sue Hines, Don Boost

   Date   May 5, 1978

   Title   Carl's Private Pain and Confession

   Publication   Modern Maturity

   Volume   32

   Page(s)   102-110

   _____

   _____

   _____

2. **Author(s) Name(s)**   Tom Grouper, Tara Bradley, Brenda Griggs, Pat Holmes

   Date   1987

   Title   Schools and the new wave of technology

   Publication   Life in the Twenty First Century

   Volume   #67

   Page(s)   34-45

_____

_____

_____

3. **Author(s) Name(s)**   Richard Eden

   Date   1990

   Title   Computers Made Easy

   Publisher   Allyn & Bacon

   Location   Boston, MA

_____

_____

_____

4. **Author(s) Name(s)**   K. E. Kane (Ed.)

   Date   1967

   Title   If Ears Could Talk and Eyes Could

                                             Hear

   Publisher   Conan/Bass

   Location   Dallas, Texas

_____

_____

_____

5. **Author(s) Name(s)**   Timothy Bronze

    Date   1990

    Title   Time, Space, and the Reality of

                               Life (rev. ed.)

    Publisher   Tisane Publishers

    Location   New York City, New York

    _____

    _____

    _____

6. **Author(s) Name(s)**   Jim Gains, William A. Lake, Paula

                               Shorts (Eds.)

    Date   1991

    Title   What Is reality?

    Publisher   Cohn Publishers

    Location   San Francisco, CA

    _____

    _____

    _____

7. **Author(s) Name(s)**   Vonda Smith, Micky Jones, Leonard

                               Benton

    Date   1981

Title	The Art of Volunteering
Location	St. Louis, MO
Meeting Type	Poster Session
Meeting Name	Third Annual Meeting for Market Research

---

8. Author(s) Name(s)	Louise Wadley, W. L. Edwards
Date	1976
Title	An Analysis of Marital Longevity
Meeting Name	Proceedings of the National Association for Families
Volume	#11
Page(s)	Pages 1186-1192
Location	Houston, Texas / Baylor University

9. **Author(s) Name(s)**   Angel C., Vesha Edwards

   Date   2000

   Title   "Life Begins At Mid-Life"   (film)

   Publication   Total Development

   Volume   #5

10. **Author(s) Name(s)**   Wayne Edwards

    Date   1971

    Title   Life Satisfaction and Retirement

    Publication   Dissertation Abstract International 39

                                  P50102

    Affiliation   University of Michigan

11. Author(s) Name(s)	Heaven Conn, Heather M. Conn, Brittany Conn
Date	1991
Title	"Rivalry Among Siblings: The Influence of Having Twin Sisters"
Publication	The Journal of Child Psychology
Volume	Volume 11
Page(s)	Pages 35 - 48

12. Author(s) Name(s)   Inge Schmidt and Zola Cranem

Date   1981

Title   In Search of Ethnic Heritage

Publication   American Heritage

Editor(s)   Bob Rogers, Greta Stewart

Page(s)   Pages 111-120

Publisher   Marks

Location   New York City

EXAMPLE APA MANUSCRIPT

The following paper, "Attitudes Towards Disabled Individuals as Influenced by Gender and Disability Type," by Jimmy L. Widdifield, Jr., is a research paper in APA style.

*The headers for this manuscript are missing so that the correct page numbers for the text will follow in sequence.

Attitudes Towards Disabled Individuals as

Influenced by Gender and Disability Type

Jimmy L. Widdifield, Jr.

University of Central Oklahoma

Abstract

The purpose of this study is to determine the attitude displayed toward permanently and temporarily physically disabled individuals and whether gender was an influencing factor. Participants viewed a variety of video vignettes depicting different levels of disability and then rated the confederate in the vignette on competency, knowledge, and how comfortable interaction would be with the confederate. These characteristics were combined to make a composite score. Analysis of the composite score indicated no negative attitude was present toward the confederate, regardless of disability and participant gender. However, when the characteristics were individually analyzed, a significant interaction was found for knowledge and a main effect for gender in the comfortability condition.

Attitudes Towards Disabled Individuals as

Influenced by Gender and Disability Type

A multitude of research has centered on discrimination based on age, race, and sex. More recently though, research on discriminatory attitudes has focused on the disabled, and more importantly, the physically disabled. This research has found that a negative attitude is held by able-bodied individuals towards the physically disabled population (Ficten & Amsel, 1986). Also, Ryan (1981) found that the physically disabled are presumed to be inferior on some dimensions and not others due to the disability and depending on the situation and context. As more physically disabled individuals are encountered in work and academic settings, it is important that society understands what kind of individuals they are and are not. Disabled people are like anyone else, with the exception of their specific disability. They are not helpless but are able to lead relatively normal lives—they marry, have children, own homes and automobiles, and pursue professional and academic careers.

Physical disability can be defined as an imputed physical defect or imperfection that is assumed to limit the capacity of an individual to engage in "normal" physical activity (Ryan, 1981). Physical disabilities are present in one of two forms, permanent or temporary. For the purpose of this study, permanent physical disability is one in which individuals are immobile due to paralysis and are thus confined to wheelchair. Temporary physical disability is a condition in which individuals have incurred an injury and must utilize a wheelchair until healing has taken place. The point of this study is to determine whether negative attitudes are present towards these two forms of physical disability and whether gender has an influence on these attitudes. Also, this study is a replication of a previous study done by Ford and Callicoat in 1991, which focused on negative attitudes towards individuals with a permanent disability. It is important to note that evaluations of the physically disabled can be more extreme than those of able-bodied individuals (Bailey, 1991).

Ford and Callicoat (1991) conducted research on attitudes towards disabled individuals. The researchers presented a confederate in one of three experimental conditions utilizing a wheelchair. These conditions depicted the confederate to be permanently, temporarily, or not disabled. Participants were asked to rate the confederate on competence, helpfulness, and how comfortable interaction with the confederate was. What the researchers found was that a negative attitude did exist in conditions when the wheelchair was present. Also discovered was that females gave fewer positive responses than males.

Negative attitudes towards physically disabled individuals have also been found in several other studies. Stovall and Sedlacek (1983) found the expression of negative attitudes towards physically disabled individuals. Here, participants formed negative attitudes to physically disabled individuals depending on the level of disability (permanent or temporary) and the situation in which the disabled person was encountered. Situations in which close contact with a disabled person was required revealed the existence of negative attitudes. Close contact here could be defined as a personal relationship. However, researchers also found that a positive attitude existed towards physically disabled individuals in academic settings and that females reacted more positively towards physically disabled individuals. Royal and Roberts (1987) also found that females expressed a more positive and accepting attitude toward individuals with a physical disability than did males. These findings suggest that attitudes towards disabled individuals are influenced by gender.

Contact with physically disabled individuals is also avoided (Ficten and Amsel, 1986). People seem to seek out companionship and contact with other individuals they perceive as similar to themselves. This has implications that can be applied to how comfortable an individual would be interacting with a person with a disability. Ficten and Amsel (1986) also found that less socially desirable traits were attributed to physically disabled individuals. These traits were, not surprisingly, the opposite of those traits attributed to able-bodied individuals.

Another area of research that can be generalized is employment potential. Ravaud, Madiot, and Ville (1992) found that qualified able-bodied applicants were more likely than physically disabled counterparts to receive a more favorable response by potential employers. Christman and Slaten (1991), however, found that physically disabled applicants were rated more favorably than able-bodied counterparts on employment characteristics and management potential scales. No explanation has been offered as to why this discrepancy exists.

Despite the large body of research conducted on the physically disabled, one population has been overlooked—the temporarily disabled. Negative attitudes towards the permanently disabled have been firmly established, but does this attitude generalize to these individuals? It is hypothesized that temporarily physically disabled individuals will be rated higher on a combination of characteristics than physically disabled individuals. Also being hypothesized is that gender of the participant will influence the ratings ascribed.

Method

Participants

Participants in this study consisted of 218 university students (females = 127, males = 91). Participants were recruited through the General Psychology Subject Pool on campus, and the mean age equaled 19.8 years. Participants received one credit for their participation, therefore aiding them to fulfill a course requirement. Treatment of participants was in accordance with the ethical standards of the American Psychological Association.

Materials

Three video vignettes were taped on a VHS tape. According to Weisel and Florian (1990) females with disabilities were regarded with a less positive attitude than males with disabilities. Therefore, a 22-year-old male confederate was used to read a script over basic cardiopulmonary resuscitation (CPR) techniques. The vignettes depicted the confederate in one of three conditions: (1) seated in a wheelchair, implying a permanent disability, (2) seated in a wheelchair with one leg extended out and wearing an ankle brace, implying a temporary disability, or (3) standing, implying no disability.

Two questionnaires were also utilized. The first was an eight-question quiz over the material presented in the video. The second was a five-question instrument concerning different components of the video and utilized Likert scales for each question. Of importance in this instrument were three questions concerning the participants' feelings about the confederate in the video. These questions focused on the perceived competency and knowledge of the confederate as well as how comfortable the participant would be interacting with the confederate. Participants were also asked to indicate their age and sex on the survey.

Procedure

Experimental sessions were conducted during a two-week period in order to obtain a sufficient number of participants. Sessions were given in 30-minute intervals, each lasting a maximum of 15 minutes. The remaining 15 minutes were used to score the participants' answers to the two questionnaires presented, as well as to re-cue the videotape. Once the participants were present and seated, credit slips were issued, and a brief explanation was given about the experimental session. Participants were told they would be viewing a brief video concerning basic CPR techniques followed by a quiz and survey. Participants were also asked to remain after they finished so that a more detailed explanation of the research could be given.

Participants then viewed one of the three video vignettes. Determination of which vignette shown was chosen randomly. After the video vignette ended, the questionnaires were administered. Once all participants finished, the researcher collected the questionnaires and credit slips. The participants were then told the current research focused on attitudes toward people with disabilities. Also, participants were invited to leave their name and address if they were interested in obtaining results of the research. Participants were then dismissed.

Results

A composite score was obtained by adding the individual scores of competency, knowledge, and how comfortable interaction would be. Data were then analyzed using a 2 (Gender) x 3 (Level of Disability) between subjects ANOVA. Table 1 shows that no significance for main effects was found as well as no interaction. Each component of the composite score was then analyzed. No significance was found in the competency component. However, a significant interaction F, $(2, 212) = 5.525$, $p < 0.0046$ was found between gender and level of disability (see Figure 2). Simple effects analysis was performed to determine where the difference would be found. Table 2a shows that significance was found at Gender at Permanent F, $(1, 212) = 5.460$, $p < 3.890$ and Disability at Male F, $(2, 212) = 3.760$, $p < 3.040$. Gender at Permanent showed a lower mean for females ($M = 7.456$) than for males ($M = 9.936$). Means for Disability at Male showed the permanent condition highest ($M = 9.936$), followed by N/A ($M = 7.350$) and temporary ($M = 7.333$). Significance was also found for the comfortability component for the Gender factor (F, $(1, 212) = 4.100$, $p < 0.0441$). Means here reveal female = 9.696 and males = 8.545 (see Table 3).

Discussion

The hypotheses of current research were (1) a more negative attitude would be present in the permanent physical disability condition and no negative attitude would exist in the temporary disability condition or N/A condition and (2) gender would influence attitudes attributed to the permanent physical disability condition. Findings for the overall composite score showed that a negative attitude was not present toward the permanent condition or the other two levels of disability. Also, gender had no influence on attitudes displayed toward the confederate in the permanent physical disability condition for the composite score. When the composite score was broken into its components of competency, knowledge, and how likely comfortable interaction would be, some interesting results were found. An interaction between gender and level of disability was present within the knowledge component. Analyses found that males perceived the permanently disabled confederate to be more knowledgeable than did females and that males perceived the permanently disabled confederate to more knowledgeable than the temporarily or non-disabled confederate. Females rated themselves to be more likely to interact with the confederate without regard to level of disability.

Results of this study seem to follow the inconsistency of previous research. Ford and Callicoat's (1991) findings suggested that a negative attitude did exist towards the permanently disabled concerning knowledge, helpfulness, and how comfortable interaction would be between participants and someone who is permanently and physically disabled. In addition to this finding, they also found females gave less positive responses than did males. In contrast, no negative attitude was found toward the permanently disabled in the current study. Another inconsistency with Ford and Callicoat's findings is current research found that males were more likely than females to perceive the permanently disabled as more knowledgeable. Even within the male group, the permanently disabled were perceived as more knowledgeable than the other two levels of disability, temporary and non-disabled.

Findings of this study are also inconsistent with research done by Stovall and Sedlacek (1983), Royal and Roberts (1983), and Ficten and Amsel (1986). These studies all found some degree of negative attitude expressed against the physically disabled. Stovall and Sedlacek's findings and current findings are inconsistent for the effects of gender; previous research found females to be more positive than males towards the permanently physically disabled. The current study found somewhat of the opposite with males responding more favorably than females. This same inconsistency is also found when looking at Royal and Robert's previous research (1987). Ficten and Amsel (1983) reported findings that contact with the physically disabled is often avoided. Current findings are interesting concerning this issue. Females were found to be more comfortable interacting with the confederate no matter the level of disability, suggesting that contact towards the permanently disabled confederate is not avoided significantly.

Findings of this study can also be compared to research done or disability and employment. As the permanently disabled are seen as more knowledgeable, as indicated by this study, results are consistent with research done by Ravaud, Madiot, and Ville (1992) as well as research done by Christman and Slaten (1991).

With previous research being inconsistent and findings of this study not agreeing or disagreeing with that previous research, it is difficult to state that a negative attitude toward the physically disabled (permanent or temporary) exists. Why do these inconsistencies exist? Possible explanations could be the level of interaction with the disabled and/or personal experience of being disabled. Ficten and Amsel (1986) found that contact with the disabled is avoided. This alone could perpetuate a negative attitude because absence of interaction does not allow people to get to know the disabled on a personal level, beyond the stereotypes.

The finding of no significance in this study could be due to methodological effects. The video vignettes showed the confederate reading from a script; this alone could affect how participants perceived the confederate. Also, participants were left to assume the confederate was either permanently or temporarily physically disabled. Allowing for this assumption could have led the participants to reach the wrong conclusion, thus interfering with the rating of the confederate.

Findings of this study could be viewed in several ways. Finding that no negative attitude exists toward the disabled could imply that mainstreaming efforts to curb discrimination are showing success. Of interest was that males responded more favorably than females toward the disabled. Historically, females have responded more favorably to disadvantaged groups, thus leaving this researcher to conclude again that mainstreaming efforts have been successful with males. Further research could focus on the differences between males and females.

References

Bailey, J. W. (1991). Evaluation of a task partner who does or does not have a physical disability: Response amplification or sympathy effect? [CD-ROM]. *Rehabilitation Psychology, 36* (2), 99-110. Abstract from: WinSpurs: PsychLIT Item: 1992-05957-001

Christman, L. A., & Slaten, B. L. (1991). Attitudes toward people with disabilities and judgment of employment potential. *Perceptual and Motor Skills, 72* (2), 467-475.

Ficten, C. S. & Amsel, R. (1986). Trait attributions about college students with a physical disability: Circumplex analyses and methodological issues. *Journal of Applied Social Psychology, 16* (5), 410-427.

Ford & Callicoat (1991, May). *Effect of perceived handicap of competency of the instructor.* Poster session presented at the biannual Student Poster Session, Edmond, OK.

Ravaud, J. F., Madiot, B., & Ville, I. (1992). Discrimination towards disabled people seeking employment. *Social Science and Medicine, 35* (8), 951-958.

Royal, G. P., & Roberts, M. C. (1987). Student's perceptions of and attitudes toward disabilities: A comparison of twenty conditions. *Journal of Clinical Child Psychology, 16* (2), 122-132.

Ryan, K. M. (1981). Developmental differences in reactions to the physically disabled. *Human Development, 24* (4), 240-256.

Stovall, C., & Sedlacek, W. E. (1983). Attitudes of male and female university students with different physical disabilities. *Journal of College Student Personnel, 27* (4), 39-47.

Weisel, A., & Florian, V. (1990). Same- and cross-gender attitudes toward persons with a physical disabilities [CD-ROM]. *Rehabilitation Psychology, 35* (4). Abstract from: WinSpurs: PsychLIT Item: 1991-27992-001

Appendix

- **Figure Captions**

- **Figures**

- **Tables**

- **LabStat Data Analyses Printouts** *(not presented)*

- **Data Summary Information** *(not presented)*

- **Vignette Quiz** *(not presented)*

- **Instructor/Confederate Survey** *(not presented)*

- Figure 1: Graph of Composite Score means in relation to Gender and Level of Disability.

- Figure 2: Graph of Knowledge Score means in relation to Gender and Level of Disability.

  Results show a significant interaction between Gender and Level of Disability.

- Figure 3: Graph of Comfortability Score means in relation to Gender and Level of Disability.

  Results show a main effect for Gender.

- Table 1: 2 x 2 between subjects ANOVA for Composite Scores.

- Table 2: 2 x 2 between subjects ANOVA for Knowledge Scores.

- Table 2a: Simple Effects analysis of Knowledge Scores.

- Table 3: 2 x 2 between subjects ANOVA for Comfortability Scores.

FIGURE 1

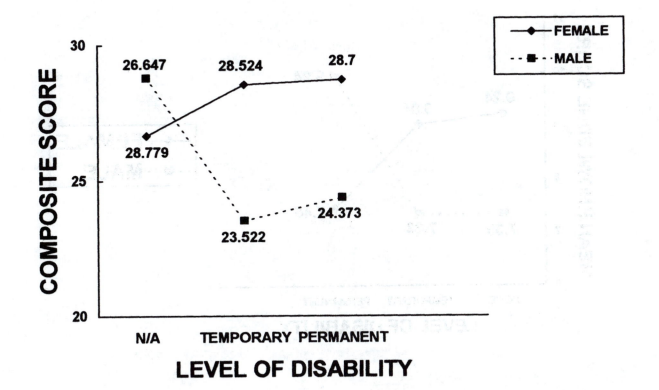

FIGURE 2

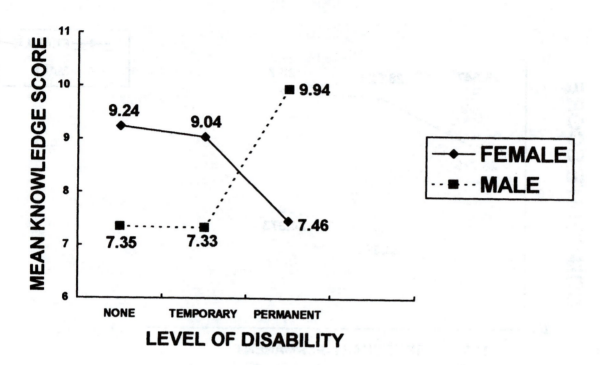

FIGURE 3

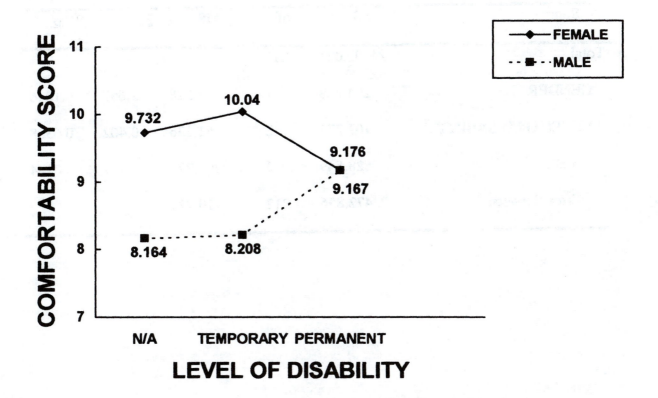

TABLE 1 Composite Scores

Source	SS	df	MS	F	p
Total	24409.021	217			
GENDER	294.228	1	294.228	2.657	0.1046
LEVEL OF DISABILITY	102.273	2	51.136	0.462	0.6308
A x B	528.549	2	264.274	2.387	0.0944
Error Between	23472.856	212	110.721		

TABLE 2 Knowledge Scores

Source	SS	df	MS	F	p
Total	4220.994	217			
GENDER	7.126	1	7.126	0.378	0.5395
LEVEL OF DISABILITY	9.785	2	4.896	0.259	0.7718
A x B	208.439	2	104.219	5.525	0.0046
Error Between	399.182	212	18.864		

TABLE 2a <u>Simple Effects of Knowledge Scores</u>

Source	SS	<u>df</u>	MS	<u>F</u>	<u>p</u>
GENDER	216.09	3			
at Permanent	103.01	1	103.01	5.46	3.89
at Temporary	60.53	1	60.53	3.21	3.89
at N/A	52.55	1	52.55	2.79	3.89
LEVEL OF DISABILITY	213.08	4			
at Female	71.27	2	35.64	1.89	3.04
at Male	141.81	2	70.91	3.76	3.04
Error Between	3999.18	212	18.86		

TABLE 3 <u>Comfortability Scores</u>

Source	SS	df	MS	F	p
Total	3487.967	217			
GENDER	65.425	1	65.425	4.100	0.0441
LEVEL OF DISABILITY	1.854	2	0.927	0.058	0.9436
A x B	32.672	2	16.336	1.024	0.3610
Error Between	3383.179	212	15.958		

Modern Language Association

(MLA) Writing Format

WHY DOCUMENT?

When using the words or ideas of someone else, you must give credit to your source. If you fail to identify the source of the words or ideas of someone else, you are plagiarizing. Plagiarism is a form of theft—the plagiarist steals the words or ideas of someone else and claims them for his or her own. To avoid such theft, you have three options: direct quotation, summary, or paraphrase.

DIRECT QUOTATION

When you quote a source directly, you must be accurate, copying not only the words but also the mechanical aspects (for instance, punctuation and capitalization) exactly as the original shows them. The only exception is hyphenation due to line endings. Quotation marks signal to your reader that everything enclosed within them are the words of someone else.

If you need to add anything to the direct quote, you may do so by enclosing your words in square brackets ([]). The brackets indicate to your reader that the words within them are yours and not part of the quotation. If you want to delete any part of the quote, you may do so by enclosing ellipses (three periods) in square brackets ([. . .]). There is no space between the opening bracket and the first ellipsis point or the last ellipsis point and the closing bracket; there is, however, a space on either side of the middle ellipsis point.

SOME WHAT-IFS

- If your brackets occur in the middle of a sentence, no matter whether you are adding words or using ellipses, be sure to leave a space on the outside of each bracket.

- If the quotation includes punctuation that would fall after your brackets, place that punctuation immediately after the closing bracket (with no space between the bracket and the punctuation).

- If you are removing a sentence or more after a complete sentence, place the brackets after the period ending the previous sentence.

- If your brackets occur at the end of a sentence, conclude the sentence with a period immediately outside the closing bracket.

- If your quote concludes with brackets, place the closing quotation marks immediately after the closing bracket, add the parenthetical reference, and conclude with a period.

ORIGINAL

Fourscore and seven years ago, our forefathers brought forth upon this continent a new nation, conceived in liberty and dedicated to the proposition that all men are created equal. Now we are engaged in a great civil war, testing whether that nation, or any nation so conceived and so dedicated, can long endure. We are met on a great battlefield of that war. We have come to dedicate a portion of that field, as a final resting place for those who here gave their lives that that nation might live. It is altogether fitting and proper that we should do this. (Lincoln, Gettysburg Address)

DIRECT QUOTATION WITH INFORMATION ADDED AND DELETED

"Fourscore and seven [87] years ago," begins Lincoln, "our forefathers brought forth on this continent a new nation [. . .] dedicated to the proposition that all men are created equal" (Gettysburg Address).

DIRECT QUOTATION WITH ELLIPSES BETWEEN SENTENCES AND AT THE END OF A SENTENCE

Lincoln continued his dedication to the battlefield, "Now we are engaged in a great civil war. [. . .] We have come to dedicate a portion of that field [. . .]" (Gettysburg Address).

ANOTHER WHAT-IF

If you must use a direct quotation that takes up four or more lines of your paper, first, make sure the quotation is extremely relevant to your paper, and second, block quote it. That is, indent each line of the entire quotation one inch from the left margin and double space. Conclude the block quote with a period and then the parenthetical reference. Note that this format differs from those references for shorter passages in which the punctuation follows the parenthetical reference.

BLOCK QUOTATION

> According to popular belief, Abraham Lincoln penned the following words on the back of an envelope while riding a train:
>> Fourscore and seven years ago, our forefathers brought forth upon this continent a new nation, conceived in

liberty and dedicated to the proposition that all men
are created equal. Now we are engaged in a great civil
war, testing whether that nation, or any nation so
conceived and so dedicated, can long endure. We are met
on a great battlefield of that war. We have come to
dedicate a portion of that field, as a final resting
place for those who here gave their lives that that
nation might live. It is altogether fitting and proper
that we should do this. (Gettysburg Address)

PARAPHRASE

A paraphrase involves restating someone else's ideas in your own words, your own style, and your own sentence structure in approximately the same length as the material you are paraphrasing.

SUMMARY

A summary involves condensing someone else's ideas in your own words, style, and sentence structure.

All three—direct quotations, paraphrases, and summaries—must be documented with in-text citations.

IN-TEXT CITATIONS

To credit your sources, use parenthetical references to point to the complete bibliographic entries you include in your list of works cited at the end of your paper. The goal, then, is to point to those references as easily as possible. Thus, in your parenthetical references, remain as close to the entries in your list of works cited as possible.

Remember always to introduce the direct quotes in your paper; that is, be sure to include words of introduction, such as *according to* or *as noted by*, to designate that the words that surround those introductory words belong to someone else:

DIRECT QUOTATION WITH AUTHOR IDENTIFIED IN TEXT

According to Smith, "the amount of time spent dwelling on the past exceeds that spent on the present" (122).

DIRECT QUOTATION WITHOUT AUTHOR IDENTIFIED IN TEXT

"The amount of time spent dwelling on the past," notes one researcher, "exceeds that spent on the present" (Smith 122).

SUMMARY WITH AUTHOR IDENTIFIED IN TEXT

Smith discusses the importance of time (122).

SUMMARY WITHOUT AUTHOR IDENTIFIED IN TEXT

Time is a relevant factor today (Smith 122).

Each of these parenthetical references points to the same reference in your list of works cited:

Smith, Robert. <u>Time's Fleeting Moments</u>. Tulsa: Smithfield,

2002.

Parenthetical references take the following general form:

(Name Page) → (Thomas 144), (Jones and Fultz 111),

(Fritz, Martin, and Cripes 28-30), (Smith et al. 222)

SOME WHAT-IFS

- If you have two authors with the same last name, include the first initial for each in your
  parenthetical references to distinguish between them:

  (A. Schmidt 78), (D. Schmidt 295)

- If two authors share not only a last name but a first initial, then use the first name for each
  in your parenthetical reference:

  (Albert Harris 184), (Ann Harris 387)

- If you have two or more works by the same author, follow the author's name with a comma
  and then a shortened version of the title beginning with the first word of the title excluding
  A, An, or *The*:

  (Mays, "Short" 22), (Mays, "Longer" 324-25)

- If no author is identified, use a shortened version of the title beginning with the first word of the title excluding *A, An,* or *The*:

  ("Writer's" 75), ("Sleeping" A2)

- If the work has no page numbers, in your parenthetical citation, use only the author's name or a shortened title if no author is given.

  ("Quick")

All of the above references are fictitious, for the purpose of illustration, and refer to the following fictitious list of works cited:

Works Cited:

Harris, Albert. "Who Knows What Will Happen?" Experience

    Grows 22 (1993): 182-89.

Harris, Ann. The Future is What We Make of It. Chicago:

    Boiler, 2000.

Mays, Joan A. "The Longer Coat." Hemming Today 21 May 2001:

    324-30.

---. "A Short Version of a Long Story." Condensed Soup 12

    Feb. 1998: 20-31.

"Quick Answers to Internet Questions." 16 May 1999. 21 June

    2001 <http://www.flippantanswers.com>.

Schmidt, Amy. "Jokes and their Punchlines." HaHa Quarterly

    22.3 (1999): 77-80.

Schmidt, David. <u>Creating Problems: A New Solution</u>. Dallas:

    Tiger, 2001.

"Sleeping Dogs Lie." <u>Bean Blossom Gazette</u> [Bean Blossom,

    IN] 31 May 2001: A2.

"A Writer's Attempts at Editing." <u>Great Flops</u> Mar. 1992:

    74-76.

MORE WHAT-IFS

- If you mention the author's name (or the title of the work when there is no author identified) in the text of the paper, you need only cite the page number(s) parenthetically.

- If you are quoting material that has been quoted by the source at which you are looking, identify in the text of the paper the original author, but in your parenthetical reference, use *qtd. in* ("quoted in") followed by the source from which you are taking the material.

- If you found the same information in two sources and want to include both of them in the same parenthetical reference, you may do so by separating the entries with a semicolon.

Again, the following example is fictitious:

Smith has argued that time escapes us (233) while Frederick claims, "Time is of the essence and must be captured" (278). Jones, however, posits the importance of living for the moment (qtd. in Lewis 343). Finally, the authors agree that time is a precious commodity (Frederick 280; Smith 177).

These citations refer to the following references in your list of works cited:

Works Cited:

Frederick, Fred F. "Transitory Moments." Today's
     Chronometers 19.2 (1999): 275-83.

Lewis, Philip J. Time's More Elegant Movements. Oklahoma
     City: Broncho, 2001.

Smith, Robert. Time's Fleeting Moments. Tulsa: Smithfield,
     2002.

WORKS CITED

<u>PRINT SOURCES:</u>

BOOKS—BASIC ENTRY

Author's Name(s). <u>Title of Book</u>. City of Publication:

    Publisher, Year of Publication.

All other entries build from the basic entry:

- Author's or Editor's Name(s) (omit titles and designations like Ph.D., M.D., and Rev., but include suffixes which are part of the name such as Jr., Sr., or III)

- "Chapter Title" or "Contribution Title" (unless introduction, preface, foreword, or afterword in which case no quotation marks)

- <u>Title of Book</u>

- Translator (Trans.), Editor (Ed.), or Compiler (Comp.)

- Edition information

- Volume information

- Series name

- City of publication

- Publisher (See XXX)

- Year of publication

- Inclusive page numbers

1. BOOK BY ONE AUTHOR

Apte, Mahadev L. Humor and Laughter: An Anthropological

Approach. Ithaca: Cornell UP, 1985.

Fry, William F., Jr. Sweet Madness: A Study of Humor. Palo

Alto: Pacific, 1963.

2. BOOK BY 2-3 AUTHORS

Andersen, Martin P., Wesley Lewis, and James Murray. The

Speaker and His Audience: Dynamic Public Speaking. New

York: Harper, 1964.

Lakoff, George, and Mark Johnson. Metaphors We Live By.

Chicago: U of Chicago P, 1980.

3. BOOK BY MORE THAN 3 AUTHORS

If a book has four or more authors, alphabetize according to the first author's last name and then use et al. *("and others") for the remaining authors' names. Alternatively, you may include all the names in the order given on the title page.*

Mindess, Harvey, et al. The Antioch Humor Test: Making

Sense of Humor. New York: Avon, 1985.

or

Mindess, Harvey, Carolyn Miller, Joy Turek, Amanda Bender,

    and Suzanne Corbin. <u>The Antioch Humor Test: Making</u>

    <u>Sense of Humor</u>. New York: Avon, 1985.

4. TWO OR MORE BOOKS BY THE SAME AUTHOR(S)

Arrange multiple entries by the same author alphabetically by title. After the first entry, use three hyphens followed by a period (---.) to show the same author. If, however, the names in any way vary or there is another author listed, you must re-enter the name. (See also 28.) When you have more than one entry by the same author, after identifying the author, alphabetize by the titles of the works, remembering to include A, An, *or* The *if it is the first word of the title but alphabetizing by the next word.*

Bergreen, Laurence. <u>As Thousands Cheer: The Life of Irving</u>

    <u>Berlin</u>. New York: Viking, 1990.

<u>Louis Armstrong: An Extravagant Life</u>. New York:

    Broadway, 1997.

Works Cited: Books with 1-3 Authors—Exercise 7

Use the following information about books by 1-3 authors to compile a Works Cited list in MLA style.

1. The Lord God made them all by James Herriot. St. Martin's Press, New York, 1981.

2. Jailbird. Kurt Vonnegut. Dell Publishing Co., Inc., New York City, NY, 1979.

3. The title is A Theory of discourse, and the subtitle is The aims of discourse. W. W. Norton and Company, New York, 1980. By James L. Kinneavy.

4. Slapstick. Written by Kurt Vonnegut. Published in New York by Dell Publishing Co., Inc., in 1976.

5. Richard Ruland and Malcolm Bradbury wrote From Puritanism to postmodernism with a subtitle of A history of American Literature. 1991. Viking. New York.

6. Sylvan Barnet, Morton Berman, and William Burto wrote A Dictionary of literary terms and published it in 1960 in Boston, Massachusetts, with Little, Brown and Company (Inc.).

WORKS CITED

5. BOOK BY A CORPORATE AUTHOR

Anheuser-Busch Companies, Inc. <u>Anheuser-Busch Companies,</u>

<u>Inc.Annual Report 1992</u>. N.p.: n.p., 1993.

Chrysler Corporation. <u>1992 Chrysler Corporation Report to</u>

<u>Shareholders</u>. N.p.: n.p., 1993.

6. BOOK WITH NO AUTHOR NAMED

The following entries are alphabetized under C and S, respectively.

<u>The Complete Annual Report and Corporate Image Planning</u>

<u>Book: 5</u>. Chicago: Alexander Communications, 1990.

<u>The Songs of Irving Berlin</u>. New York: Irving Berlin Music,

n.d.

7. EDITED BOOK

For edited books, including translations (see 11), you need to determine whose work you are

citing. If the work and words of the editor are what you are citing, list the work alphabetically by

the editor's name. If, however, the work and words of the original author are what you are citing,

list the work alphabetically by the author's name. If you start with the editor, follow the name with

ed. ("editor") and then title of the work. After the title, use By *and then the name(s) of the*

author(s) in natural order. (Also see 10 for other examples of using By *in citations.) If you start*

with the name(s) of the author(s) and then the title of the work, follow the title by its editor(s), use

Ed. ("edited by") before the name(s) of the editor(s) in natural order.

The first entry is for citing the words or idea(s) of the editors.


```
Beaver, Harold, ed. Redburn. By Herman Melville. New York:

     Penguin, 1976.

Blair, Walter, ed. Selected Shorter Writings of Mark Twain.

     By Mark Twain. Boston: Houghton, 1962.
```

The following entry is to cite the words or idea(s) of the authors.


```
Melville, Herman. Redburn. Ed. Harold Beaver. New York:

     Penguin, 1976.

Twain, Mark. "The Man That Corrupted Hadleyburg." Selected

     Shorter Writings of Mark Twain. Ed. Walter Blair.

     Boston: Houghton, 1962. 245-89.
```

8. ANTHOLOGY, COLLECTION, OR REFERENCE BOOK (INCLUDING DICTIONARIES AND ENCYCLOPEDIAS)

For well-known reference works like dictionaries and encyclopedias, do not cite the name(s) of the editor(s) or the publication information. For lesser known reference works, however, include the name(s) of the editor(s) and full publication information. If you are citing a dictionary definition, enclose the word you are citing in quotation marks followed by Def. *(for definition) and the number of the definition (if there is more than one definition given) you are citing.*

Morreall, John, ed. <u>The Philosophy of Laughter and Humor</u>.

    Albany: State U of New York P, 1987.

Thompson, G. Richard, ed. <u>Romantic Gothic Tales: 1790-1840</u>.

    New York: Harper, 1979.

"Viscous." Def. 2. <u>The American Heritage Dictionary</u>. 2nd

    coll. ed. 1982.

9. WORK IN AN EDITED BOOK BY AUTHOR(S) DIFFERENT FROM EDITOR(S)

Begin with the name(s) of the author(s) of the work you are citing and then the title of the work you are citing in quotation marks. Follow with the name of the book from which the piece comes and then the name(s) of the editor(s). Be sure to place the inclusive page numbers of the work after the period following the date of publication.

Couture, Barbara, and Jone Rymer. "Situational Exigence:

    Composing Processes on the Job by Writer's Role and

    Task Value." <u>Writing in the Workplace: New Research</u>

    <u>Perspectives</u>. Ed. Rachel Spilka. Carbondale: Southern

    Illinois UP, 1993. 4-20.

Faigley, Lester. "Nonacademic Writing: The Social

    Perspective." <u>Writing in Nonacademic Settings</u>. Ed. Lee

    Odell and Dixie Goswami. New York: Guilford, 1985.

    231-48.

10. INTRODUCTION, PREFACE, FOREWORD, OR AFTERWORD

Alphabetize by the author(s) of the introduction, preface, foreword, or afterword. Follow the author's name with the name of the section you are citing (Introduction, Preface, Foreword, or Afterword—neither in quotation marks nor underlined). Continue with the title of the work. Follow the title with the word By *and then the author's name. If the author of the work is the same as the author of the section you are citing, use only the author's last name. Continue with the publication information. Conclude the entry with the inclusive page numbers of the section you are citing.*

Dubos, René. Introduction. <u>Anatomy of an Illness as Perceived by the Patient</u>. By Norman Cousins. New York: Norton, 1979. 11-23.

Inhelder, Bärbel. Foreword. <u>Piaget's Theory of Intellectual Development: An Introduction</u>. By Herbert Ginsburg and Sylvia Opper. Englewood Cliffs: Prentice, 1969. vii-viii.

11. TRANSLATION

Alphabetize by the author of the work you are citing. After the title of the work, add Trans. *(for "translated by") followed by the name(s) of the translator(s). Continue with the publication information.*

Aristotle. <u>The Rhetoric and the Poetics of Aristotle</u>.

    Trans. W. Rhys Roberts and Ingram Bywater. New York:

    Random, 1954.

Ibsen, Henrik. <u>Peer Gynt</u>. Trans. Rolf Fjelde. New York:

    Signet, 1964.

Works Cited: Works in Edited Books—Exercise 8

Use the following information to compile a Works Cited list in MLA style.

1. The title is Writing in the academic disciplines, 1870-1990. The subtitle is A curricular history. The author is David R. Russell. Southern Illinois University Press, Carbondale and Edwardsville, Illinois, 1991. You are quoting from the foreword, which appears on pages ix-xi, by Elaine P. Maimon.

2. Herman Melville's poem Monody, which appears on pp. 593-594 of The Portable Melville, edited by Jay Leyda. Penguin Books. New York. 1952.

3. The title of the collection in which you found the Dylan Thomas poem And Death Shall Have No Dominion (on page 77) is The Collected Poems of Dylan Thomas. New Directions in New York published the book in 1953.

4. Patricia Bizzell and Bruce Herzberg edited a book with the title of The Rhetorical tradition and subtitle of Readings from classical times to the present. You are citing Richard Weaver's Language is sermonic, which starts on page 1044 and goes to page 1054. The book was published in Boston in 1990 by Bedford Books.

5. You are citing W. H. Auden's introduction to the book on Edgar Allan Poe that Auden edited. The title of the book is Poe: Selected prose and Poetry. The book is a revised edition published by Holt, Rinehart and Winston in New York in 1964. Auden's introduction starts on page v and continues to page xvii.

WORKS CITED

12. CROSS-REFERENCE

If you are citing from more than one work in a collection or anthology, you can cross-reference the work by creating a complete entry alphabetized by the editor(s) name(s) and then for each cross-reference, state the author and title of each piece followed by the last name(s) of the editor(s) and the inclusive page numbers. If a work is translated, identify the translator(s,) after the title of the translated piece.

Boskin, Joseph. "Our Private Laughter: American Cynicism
    and Optimism." Nilsen 213-20.

Cisneros, Sandra. "My Name." Nilsen 12.

Dunkling, Leslie. "Making a Name for Yourself." Nilsen 30-
    33.

Keillor, Garrison. "The Speeding Ticket." Nilsen 273-77.

Nilsen, Alleen Pace, ed. <u>Living Language: Reading,</u>
    <u>Thinking, and Writing</u>. Boston: Allyn, 1999.

Smilgis, Martha. "The Celebs' Golden Mouthpiece." Nilsen
    331-33.

13. EDITION

When you are using an edition other than a first edition, it is customary to make note of the subsequent edition in your entry. The title page of the work usually indicates the edition. If none is identified, it is generally safe to assume the work is a first edition, so you need not indicate an edition in this case. Some editions are numbered (2nd ed., 3rd ed., etc.), some are revised (Rev. ed.), and some are shortened or abridged (Abr. ed.). Some editions are even designated by year (2001 ed.). Any identifying information about the edition appears after the name(s) of the editor(s), translator(s), and/or compiler(s).

Fromkin, Victoria, and Robert Rodman. <u>An Introduction to</u>
   <u>Language</u>. 5th ed. Fort Worth: Harcourt, 1993.

Klammer, Thomas P., and Muriel R. Schultz. <u>Analyzing</u>
   <u>English Grammar</u>. 2nd ed. Boston: Allyn, 1996.

14. POEM

Treat a poem exactly like a book if it is a long, individually published work. Most poems, however, are considerably shorter and are published as part of a collection. When the latter is the case, treat the title of the poem exactly as you would the title of a chapter in a book or an article in a periodical.

Aiken, Conrad. "Dear Uncle Stranger." <u>The Norton Anthology</u>
   <u>of Modern Poetry</u>. Ed. Richard Ellmann and Robert
   O'Clair. New York: Norton, 1973. 484-85.

Eliot, T. S. "The Old Gumbie Cat." <u>The Complete Poems and</u>
   <u>Plays: 1909-1950</u>. San Diego: Harcourt, 1971. 150-51.

15. MULTIVOLUME WORK

If a work appears in more than one volume and you are using more than one volume, cite the total number of volumes after the title of the work. (If the work appears in an edition other than the first, cite the number of volumes after the edition.) If, however, you are citing from only one volume of the collection, state the volume number after the title of the work. If the collection has been

published over a number of years, use the inclusive years as your date of publication.

Hart, B. H. Liddell. <u>History of the Second World War</u>. 2
     vols. New York: Capricorn, 1972.

Lyons, John. <u>Semantics</u>. 2 vols. New York: Cambridge UP,
     1977.

Witt, Mary Ann Frese, et al. <u>The Humanities: Cultural Roots</u>
     <u>and Continuities</u>. 6th ed. Vol. 1. Boston: Houghton,
     2001.

16. BOOK IN A SERIES

For a book in a series, identify the name of the series (neither underlined nor in quotation marks)
followed by the volume number after the title of the book. If Series *is part of the name of the series,*
abbreviate it as Ser.

Raskin, Victor. <u>Semantic Mechanisms of Humor</u>. Synthese
     Language Library Texts and Studies in Linguistics and
     Philosophy. 24. Dordrecht: Reidel, 1985.

17. REPUBLISHED BOOK

If you are citing a book that has been republished, identify the original year of publication
followed by a period after the title of the book. Continue with the publication information for the
text you are using.

106

Gaskell, Elizabeth. Mary Barton. 1848. New York: Penguin,

    1970.

Greig, J. Y. T. The Psychology of Laughter and Comedy.

    1923. New York: Cooper Square, 1969.

18. UNPUBLISHED DISSERTATION

A reference to an unpublished dissertation begins with the author's name and is followed by the

title of the dissertation in quotation marks. After the title, use Diss. *to indicate* dissertation *and*

then the abbreviated name of the university (see XX) at which the dissertation was written,

followed by a comma, followed by the year in which the dissertation was composed, and concluded

with a period.

Carrell, David Allen. "The Ethos of Two Corporate Annual

    Reports: A Rhetorical Analysis of the Visual and

    Discursive Aspects." Diss. Purdue U, 1994.

Haiman, Franklyn. "An Experimental Study of the Effects of

    Ethos in Public Speaking." Diss. Northwestern U, 1948.

19. GOVERNMENT PUBLICATION

Because government publications come from many sources, first identify the government (for

instance, United States *or* Oklahoma) *and then the agency or branch from which the document*

came. For references to the Congressional Record, simply use Cong. Rec. *followed by the date*

and page numbers. (In the first entry, the S *before the page numbers indicates* Senate.)

Cong. Rec. 18 May 2000. S4122-70.

United States. Dept. of Health and Human Services. Surgeon

General's Workshop on Drunk Driving: Proceedings.

Rockville: U. S. Dept. of Health and Human Services,

1989.

20. PUBLISHED CONFERENCE PROCEEDINGS

Knuf, Joachim, ed. Unity and Diversity: Proceedings of the

Fourth International Conference on Narrative, October

1995, U of Kentucky. Lexington: College of

Communications and Information Studies of U of

Kentucky, 1996.

21. PAMPHLET

Treat a pamphlet exactly like a book.

22. A BOOK WITHOUT PUBLICATION INFORMATION AND/OR PAGINATION

Occasionally, a book is published without the city of publication, publisher's name, and/or date of

publication provided. Some books are printed without page numbers. When you can approximate,

for instance, a year of publication, enclose it in brackets (for instance [2000] or [2001?], the

question mark clearly indicating a guess) to show that you have added the information. Use the

following abbreviations to indicate gaps in information. (See also 5 and 6.)

n.p.	No place of publication given
n.p.	No publisher identified
n.d.	No date of publication indicated
n. pag.	No pagination included

The following are fictional references to illustrate how to include the above information:

```
Jones, D. "Who Wants to Know What?" No Records to Keep.

     N.p.: n.p., [2001?], n. pag.

Smith, Fred. Publishing with Freedom. N.p.: n.p., n.d.
```

ARTICLES

BASIC ENTRY:

```
Author's Name(s). "Article Title." Title of Publication

     Publication information: page numbers.
```

All other entries build from the basic entry:

- Author's Name(s)

- "Chapter Title" or "Contribution Title"

- Title of Publication

- Volume information for scholarly journals

- Issue number if necessary (see 27)

- Date of publication (abbreviate all months except May, June, and July)
- Inclusive page numbers

A note on unsigned entries

If no author is identified, alphabetize using the title of the article. Do not alphabetize using A, An, *or* The *if it is the first word of the title. Include* A, An, *or* The, *but alphabetize using the next word.*

23. NEWSPAPER ARTICLE

After the author's name (if given) and the title of the article (in quotation marks), identify the name of the newspaper as it appears on the masthead of the paper except ignore and delete A, An, *or* The *if it is the first word of the title of the newspaper. If the city of publication is not clear from the title of the newspaper, enclose it in brackets (but do not underline it) after the title of the newspaper. If a specific edition is included on the masthead (such as* late ed.*), specify it after the date, separating the date from the edition with a comma. If the article appears on consecutive pages, identify the page numbers after a colon after the date, and conclude the entry with a period. If, however, the article does not appear on consecutive pages, identify the page on which the article begins, and follow that number with a plus sign (+) and then a period (with no space between the + and the period).*

Calaway, Nancy, and Lesley Téllez. "Horse Owners Intensify

    Security: Meat Demand Overseas Cited." <u>Dallas Morning</u>

    <u>News</u> 17 June 2001: 31A+.

Medley, Robert. "Electricity May Be Out Awhile." <u>Daily</u>

    <u>Oklahoman</u> [Oklahoma City] 30 May 2001: A1+.

24. MAGAZINE ARTICLE

For magazines published every week or two weeks, use the full date (day followed by month followed by year). For magazines published every month or two months, give the month and year. In both cases, abbreviate month(s) other than May, June, and July. Follow the same rules for newspaper articles for page references.

Gopnik, Adam. "A Walk on the High Line: The Allure of a

    Derelict Railroad Track in Spring." <u>New Yorker</u> 21 May

    2001: 44-49.

Rosing, Norbert. "Bear Beginnings: New Life on the Ice."

    <u>National Geographic</u> Dec. 2000: 30-39.

Sanders, Stephanie. "New School? No Sweat!" <u>Girls' Life</u>

    Aug.-Sep. 2000: 70+.

25. A LETTER TO THE EDITOR OR AN EDITORIAL

For both newspapers and magazines, designate a letter to the editor with Letter *(without quotation marks or underlining) following the name of the writer. For an editorial, add* Editorial *(without quotation marks or underlining) after the title of the editorial. If the editorial is signed, begin with the writer's name. If it is unsigned, begin with the title of the editorial. Continue your citation for*

the publication.

Beyerl, Paul. Letter. <u>Time</u> 31 July 2000: 8.

"The Global Warming Gap." Editorial. <u>New York Times</u> 17 June
     2001, natl. ed., sec. 4: 14.

Raskin, Robin. "The Good Life, 2001." Editorial. <u>Family PC</u>
     July 2001: 17.

26. REVIEW

To document a review, begin with the name of the reviewer (if provided) followed by the title of the

review (if it has a name). After the title, add Rev. of *("review of"—neither underlined nor in*

quotation marks) and then the title of the piece that has been reviewed, a comma, and then the

author's name. (See 7 and 10 for other example usages of by.*) If there is neither a reviewer nor a*

title given, begin your citation with Rev. of *followed by the title of the reviewed work. Alphabetize*

the entry by the first word of the title of the work under review excluding A, An, *or* The. *If the*

work's editing, translation, or direction, for instance, is under review, use ed., trans., *or* dir. *in*

place of by. *Continue with the remaining bibliographic information for the source in which you*

found the review.

Bortz, Fred. "Lighting the Dark." Rev. of <u>An Intimate Look</u>
    <u>at the Night Sky</u>, by Chet Raymo. <u>Dallas Morning News</u>
    17 June 2001: 8C.

Rev. of <u>Romanticism and Its Discontents</u>, by Anita Brookner.

<u>New Yorker</u> 13 Nov. 2000: 174.

Works Cited: Newspaper and Magazine

Articles, Letters to the Editor, Editorials, and Reviews—Exercise 9

Using the following information, compile a Works Cited list following MLA style.

1. The title of the article is A murderer times four. Its subtitle is DNA clues can make life easier for cops—or tougher. The authors of the article, which appeared in the September 6, 1999, issue of Newsweek (Volume CXXXIV, Number ten) are John McCormick and Steve Rhodes. The article appears only on page 33.

2. Juliet Barker's review of John Worthen's book The Gang: Coleridge, the Hutchinsons and the Wordsworths in 1802 is called "A Year in the Life: A microhistory of an extraordinary literary collaboration." The review appeared in the April 2001 issue of The Atlantic Monthly magazine on pages 96, 97, 98.

3. You read with interest Bernadette Grey's editorial called That Age-Old Question on page four in the October 2000 issue of Working Woman.

4. On page 10 of the national edition of The New York Times on Sunday, 17 June 2001, you found Don Kirk's article Seoul Nudges North toward new talks. The article does not continue on another page.

5. "Jolie Gives Indiana Jones Run for his Money" is the title of the review by Jim Chastain, II, of the movie Lara Croft: Tomb Raider, directed by Simon West. The review appeared

on page 13A of the June 17, 2001, edition of The Edmond Sun, which is published in

Edmond, Oklahoma.

6. The letter to the editor by Brendan Walsh of Dublin, Ireland, appears on page 16 of the

February 2001 issue of The Atlantic Monthly magazine.

7. The title of the article is 2001 Coin Forecast. The subtitle is Numismatic experts look at the

year ahead. The author is Ed Reiter. You found the article in the January 2001 issue of

Coinage magazine. The article appears on pages 10, 11, and 14.

WORKS CITED

_____

_____

_____

_____

_____

_____

_____

_____

_____

_____

_____

_____

_____

_____

_____

_____

_____

_____

_____

JOURNALS

Scholarly journals either number the pages of each issue or each volume separately. (A volume usually consists of two or more issues published in the same year.) When each issue has its pages numbered separately, you need to identify the issue number as well as the volume number. When the pages in a volume are numbered continuously, identify only the volume number. Include the volume number or the volume and issue number after the title of the journal. Separate the volume and issue numbesr with a period but with no space following the period.

27. SEPARATE PAGINATION FOR EACH ISSUE

Howard, Elizabeth. "Preparing Reports in the 1990s." Public Relations Journal 36.5 (1991): 26-27.

Kellner, Douglas. "Reading Images Critically: Toward a Postmodern Pedagogy." Journal of Education 170.3 (1988): 31-52.

28. CONTINUOUS PAGINATION

Courtis, J. K. "An Investigation into Annual Report Readability and Corporate Risk-Return Relationships." Accounting and Business Research 16 (1986): 285-96.

Courtis, John K. "The Reliability of Perception-Based Annual Report Disclosure Studies." Accounting and Business Research 23 (1992): 31-43.

Zhao, Yan. "The Information-Conveying Aspect of Jokes."

HUMOR: International Journal of Humor Research 1

(1988): 279-98.

Works Cited: Journals—Exercise 10

Using the following information, compile a Works Cited list following MLA style.

1. The title of the article is Ben and Jerry scoop up credibility. The author of the article, which appeared in a 1993 issue of the Public Relations Journal (Volume 38, Number eight) is Betsy Wiesendanger. The article appears only on page 20. The journal repaginates with every issue.

2. The title of Carolyn Miller's article in the Central states Speech Journal is Technology as a form of consciousness. Its subtitle is A study of contemporary ethos. The article appeared in 1978 on pages 228 to 236. The volume number is 29, and the pages are not renumbered with each issue.

3. James A. Berlin's article appeared in Rhetoric review. Its title is Poststructuralism, cultural studies, and the composition Classroom. The subtitle of Berlin's article is Postmodern theory in practice. The article began on page 16 and ran to page 33 in the first issue of volume 11, which was published in 1992, and which does not repaginate with each issue.

4. The article called Annual report Competition, which has no author identified, begins on page 70 of a 1992 issue of Financial world. The article runs continuously to page 80. You have identified the issue number as 22 and the volume number as 161.

5.-6. You found two articles by Charles Kostelnick. Both articles were in the Journal of business and technical communication. One article is called "Typographical design, modernist aesthetics, and professional communication." It appeared in the first issue of the fourth volume, which was published in 1990, on pages five through twenty-four. The second article has a title and subtitle. The title is From pen to print, and the subtitle is "The new visual landscape of Professional communication." This article appeared in 1994, which is the eighth volume of the journal, beginning on page 91 and running to page 117. The journal of business and technical communication does not renumber its pages with each issue.

WORKS CITED

_____

_____

_____

_____

_____

_____

_____

_____

_____

_____

_____

_____

_____

_____

_____

_____

_____

_____

_____

ELECTRONIC SOURCES

Follow the same basic rules for electronic sources as you do for printed sources (books, magazines, journals, etc.) except that you must also include in the citation the most current electronic address—the Uniform Resource Locator (URL)—as well as the date you accessed the information. Be sure to enclose the URL in angled brackets (< >) and include the access mode identifier (*http, telnet, gopher, ftp, news*). In addition, provide, if possible, the date the material was originally posted (published).

BASIC ENTRY

Title of project or database. Project editor. Version
     number. Date of electronic publication or last update.
     Sponsoring institution or organization. Date accessed.
     <URL>.

29. SCHOLARLY PROJECT OR DATABASE

Begin your entry with the title of the project or database and underline it as you would a book title. Follow that information with the name of the editor(s), if provided. Then include any electronic publication information such as the version number (which is comparable to the edition of print sources), the date of publication or the most recent update, and the name of the sponsor, institution, or affiliation. Conclude your entry with the date you accessed the site and the network address of the site.

AskERIC. ERIC Clearinghouse on Information & Technology,
     Syracuse U. 19 June 2001 <http://ericir.syr.edu/>.

Folger Shakespeare Library. 7 June 2001. Folger Shakespeare

   Library. 11 June 2001 <http://www.folger.edu/>.

The Galileo Project. Ed. Albert Van Helden and Elizabeth

   Burr. 5 Aug. 1996. Rice U. 4 June 2001 <http://es.

   rice.edu/ES/humsoc/Galileo/>.

Infojump: Information for the Masses. 1999. Infojump. 8

   June 2001 <http://www.infojump.com/>.

National Women's History Project. 2001. National Women's

   History Project. 30 May 2001 <http://www.nwhp.org/>.

The Perseus Digital Library. Ed. Gregory Crane. Tufts U. 8 June

2001 <http://www.perseus.tufts.edu/>.

Project Diana: Online Human Rights Archive. 10 June 2001.

   Yale Law School. 10 June 2001 <http://www.yale.edu/

   lawweb/avalon/diana/index.html>.

Project Gutenberg: Fine Literature Digitally Re-Published.

   28 May 2001. 3 June 2001 <http://promo.net/pg/>.

30. A DOCUMENT WITHIN A SCHOLARLY PROJECT OR DATABASE

To cite a document within a scholarly project or database, treat it as you would an article in a

print journal: begin with the author's name, if given, and then the title of the work in quotation

marks. Continue as you would document a scholarly project or database, but be sure that the URL

is for the specific document to which you are referring.

Butler, Josephine E. "Truth Before Everything." Victorian

Women's Writers Project. Ed. Perry Willett. 23 June

1996. Indiana U. 10 June 2001 <http://www.indiana.

edu/~letrs/vwwp/butler/truth.html>.

"Corrections to the Collected Works of Jeremy Bentham." The

Bentham Project. Ed. Irena Nicoll. 8 June 2001. U

College London. 11 June 2001 <http://www.ucl.ac.uk/

Bentham-Project/corrections/correctn.htm>.

31. ARTICLE, LETTER, OR EDITORIAL FROM AN ONLINE PERIODICAL INCLUDING NEWSPAPERS, MAGAZINES, AND SCHOLARLY JOURNALS

Follow the recommendations above for articles, letters, and editorials in print (hard copy) except that you must add information to designate the entries as having come from electronic sources: the date you accessed the material and the network address.

Puente, Michael. "New Gridlock Woes Grip Roads in Region."

Post-Tribune (Gary, IN) 9 June 2001. 9 June 2001

<http://www.post-trib.com/cgi-bin/pto-story/news/z1/

06-09-01_z1_news_1.html>.

Rozek, Dan. "Jury Problems in Midwife Trial." Chicago Sun-

Times 3 June 2001. 8 June 2001

<http://www.suntimes.com/output/news/mid03.html>.

Zuckerman, Mortimer B. "A Time to Reap—and Sow." Editorial.

usnews.com. 4 June 2001. 9 June 2001 <http://

www.usnews.com/usnews/issue/010604/opinion/4edit.htm>.

32. ORGANIZATIONAL OR PERSONAL HOME PAGE

For organizational and personal home pages, begin your citation with the name of the organization or individual who created the home page. Follow with the title of the site, underlined, if provided. If the web page has no title, use a descriptive term such as Home page *(without underlining or quotation marks). Finish the reference as above: the date of publication or the most recent update (if available), the name of the sponsor, institution, or affiliation, the date you accessed the site, and the network address of the site.*

Andrean High School Home Page. 11 June 2001. Andrean High

    School. 15 June 2001 <http://www.andreanhs.com>.

Institute of International Education: IIE Online. Institute

    of International Education. 14 June 2001

    <http://www.iie.org>.

33. EMAIL COMMUNICATION

To include an email communication in your list of works cited, begin with the name of the sender (as you would an author), the title of the message from the subject line (if any) in quotation marks, a description of the message (such as "Email to author" without quotation marks, and the date of the message.

Canada, Cassandra J. "It's a Girl." Email to the author. 24

    Apr. 2001.

Fritz, Paul. Email to Joan Krebbs. 10 May 2001.

Works Cited: Online Publications—Exercise 11

Using the following information, compile a Works Cited list following MLA style.

1. The title of the article is Man Who Saved old tree given tree preservation award. The author is Max Showalter. The article appeared on May 25, 2001, in the Journal and Courier Online newspaper from Lafayette, Indiana. You found the material at <http://www.lafayettejc.com/news0525/0525l07.shtml> on June 3, 2001.

2. You looked at NASA's Voyager Project Home Page on June 4, 2001. It had last been updated in May 2001. The URL you used was <http://vraptor.jpl.nasa.gov/voyager/voyager.html>.

3. On June 9, 2001, you found The Orlando Project: An Integrated History of Women's Writing in the British Isles at <http://www.ualberta.ca/ORLANDO/>. Its last update was on May 2, 2001. Paul Dyck and Cathy Grant maintain the site at the University of Alberta.

4. David Mendell, a staff reporter, wrote the article called "City agency defends public arts spending: cultural Affairs books juggled," which appeared online in the Chicago Tribune on the same day you looked at the page, 9 June 2001, at <http://www.chicagotribune.com/news/metro/chicago/article/0,2669,ART-52336,FF.html>.

5. On May 21, 2001, you found the Scyld Computing Corporation's The Beowulf Project edited by Donald Becker and Phil Merkey. The last time the site at <http://www.beowulf.org/> was updated was April 27, 2001.

6. You sent email to a professor at another school to ask for information. Dr. Ralph Schmidt answered your inquiry by email on February 22, 2001.

WORKS CITED

OTHER SOURCES

34. RADIO OR TELEVISION PROGRAM

To cite a radio or television program, treat the name of the episode or segment as you would an article title by putting it in quotation marks and then underlining the title of the program. Follow the title of the program with the name of the series, if there is one, but without underlining or quotation marks. Then identify the name of the network (such as WGN or PBS), the call letters of the local station and its location (for example, KOSU, Stillwater or WTTW, Chicago), and the date of broadcast. Other information including the names of performers, editors, directors, narrators can be added. Follow the guidelines in the previous sections.

"Last Primates of Madagascar." <u>Crocodile Hunter</u>. Host Steve

       Irwin. Animal Planet. 20 June 2001.

<u>Piano Concerto in G</u>. By Maurice Ravel. Perf. Alicia de

       Larrocha. Cond. Leonard Slatkin. St. Louis Symphony.

       WFMT. Chicago. 15 Apr. 2001.

"Terror in Space: Life-Threatening Problems Aboard the

       Space Station Mir." <u>Nova</u>. PBS. OETA, Oklahoma City. 23

       June 2001.

35. INTERVIEW

There are three kinds of interviews: those published or recorded, those broadcast on television or radio, and those you conduct yourself. While the documentation style is similar for all three, there are some differences. In all cases, begin with the name of the person interviewed. If the interview is part of a larger work, treat its title, if it has one, as you would an article title by enclosing it in quotation marks and then continuing with the rest of the publication information. If the interview

has been published as a discrete entity, underline its title. If it has no title, use the word Interview

(without quotation marks or underlining). If you know the interviewer's name, you may include it

as well if the interviewer is important to your paper (for instance, Interview with Dan Rather*). For*

radio and television interviews, as with other radio and television broadcasts, add the name of the

network, the call letters of the local station, and the date of broadcast. For interviews that you

conduct yourself, follow the name of the person you interviewed with the type of interview

*(*Telephone interview *or* Personal interview*) and the date of the interview.*

Carter, Jimmy. Interview with Lisa Simeone. <u>Weekend All</u>

    <u>Things Considered</u>. Natl. Public Radio. KOSU,

    Stillwater. 17 June 01.

Heit, Siegfried E. Personal interview. 8 Sept. 2000.

Smith, Sarah Thomas. Telephone interview. 9 Mar. 2001.

36. VISUAL RECORDING

Begin with the title of the work, underlined, and follow the title with the name of the director, the

distributor, and the year of release. If relevant, you may want to include the names of

performer(s), writer(s), and/or producer(s), with appropriate designations (such as Perf. *or* Prod.*)*

between the title and the distributor. For DVDs, laser disc, and videocassette releases, begin as

you would other visual recordings, including the original date of release but excluding the

distributor of the original release. After the original date of release, note the medium (for instance,

DVD, Filmstrip, *or* Videocassette—*without quotation marks or underlining) followed by the*

current distributor and the year of release.

Casablanca. Dir. Michael Curtiz. Perf. Humphrey Bogart,

    Ingrid Bergman, and Sidney Greenstreet. 1943.

    Videocassette. Warner Home Video, 1998.

Cast Away. Dir. Robert Zemeckis. Perf. Tom Hanks and Helen

    Hunt. 2000. DVD. 20th Cent. Fox Home Entertainment,

    2001.

Dr. Dolittle 2. Dir. Steve Carr. Perf. Eddie Murphy and

    Jeffrey Jones. 20th Cent. Fox, 2001.

37. CONFERENCE PRESENTATION, LECTURE, OR ADDRESS

Begin your reference with the speaker's name, followed by the title of the speech (if it has a title)

in quotation marks. If the speech has no title, provide an appropriate designation such as Lecture,

Keynote speech, *or* Address *(neither underlined nor in quotation marks) after the speaker's name.*

Continue the reference with the name of the meeting and sponsoring organization (if possible and

if not clear from the name of the meeting), the location, and the date.

Davies, Christie. "Jokes, Soccer, Sadomasochism, and

    Aggression in Britain and Possibly America." Intl.

    Soc. for Humor Studies Conf. U of Central Oklahoma,

    Edmond. 11 July 1997.

38. ADVERTISEMENT

To refer to an advertisement, use the name of the company, product, or institution being advertised

where you would have the author's name. Then add Advertisement, *without quotation marks or underlining. Continue with the remaining publication information.*

IBM ThinkPad. Advertisement. <u>Computer Shopper</u>. July 2001:

    69-71.

New York Design Center. Advertisement. <u>Town and Country</u>

    June 2000: 137.

39. CARTOON

To refer to a cartoon, begin with the cartoonist's name followed by the title of the cartoon, if it has

a title, in quotation marks. Then add Cartoon, *without quotation marks of underlining. Continue*

with the remaining publication information.

Davis, Jim. "Garfield." Cartoon. <u>Daily Oklahoman</u> [Oklahoma

    City] 23 June 2001: 6-B.

Ziegler, Jack. Cartoon. <u>New Yorker</u> 7 May 2001: 77.

ABBREVIATIONS

MLA style uses a number of abbreviations regularly. Below are some guidelines and common abbreviations used in MLA documentation.

Publishers' Names

When citing the names of publishers, MLA shortens or abbreviates them.

Omit articles (*A, An,* and *The*) and business designations and abbreviations such as *Corporation, Co., Corp., Inc.,* etc. Also omit words like *Books* (Penguin Books is simply Penguin), *House* (Random House is simply Random), *Press* (except with university presses, see below), *Publishers,* and the like.

Abbreviate *University* as U and *Press*, **only** for a university press, as P.

State University of New York Press → State U of New York P

Yale University Press → Yale UP

If the publisher's name is that of a person, like W. W. Norton, use only the last name (Norton). If the publisher's name includes a list of names, use only the first in the list. For instance, for Harper & Row, use only Harper. For Houghton Mifflin, use only Houghton.

Use standard abbreviations such as MLA for The Modern Language Association of America, ERIC for Educational Resources Information Center, and APA for the American Psychological

Association.

Some common abbreviations follow:

For	Use
Allyn and Bacon	*Allyn*
April	Apr.
August	Aug.
Charles Scribner's Sons	Scribner's
College	coll.
Compiler(s)/Compiled by	comp.
Conference	conf.
Congress	Cong.
Congressional Record	*Cong. Rec.*
December	Dec.
Director/Directed by	dir.
Dissertation Abstracts International	*DAI*
Edition	ed.
Editor(s)/Edited by	ed.
February	Feb.
Government Printing Office	GPO
Harper & Row, Publishers, Inc.	Harper
HarperCollins Publishers, Inc.	Harper

Holt, Rinehart and Winston, Inc.	Holt
Houghton Mifflin Company	Houghton
International	intl.
January	Jan.
Little, Brown and Company, Inc.	Little
McGraw-Hill, Inc.	McGraw
The National Council of Teachers of English	NCTE
National	natl.
No date of publication	n.d.
No identified publisher	n.p.
No pagination	n. pag.
No place of publication	n.p.
November	Nov.
October	Oct.
Prentice-Hall, Inc.	Prentice
Purdue University Press	Purdue UP
Random House, Inc.	Random
Section	sec.
September	Sept.
Simon and Schuster, Inc.	Simon
Society	St. Martin's
Thomas Nelson Publishers	Nelson
Translator/Translated by	trans.

University	U (for documentation) or univ. (otherwise)
University Press	UP (used in references)
W. W. Norton and Co., Inc.	Norton

FORMATTING A PAPER IN MLA STYLE

MLA style allows two ways to format a paper: with or without a separate title page. When a formal outline is included with the paper, MLA requires a title page. (For a sample title page and formal outline, see the model paper below.) Without a title page, all the necessary identifying information is in the upper left corner on the first page of the paper in the following order:

```
Your Name

Professor's Name

Course

Date

                    Title
    (The title is in the same font as the rest of the paper:
    no bold, italics, underlining, and/or quotation marks.)
```

Margins

Use a one-inch margin on all four sides of the paper. In the upper right corner, one-half inch from the top of the page, insert your last name followed by one space and the page number on each page, including the `Works Cited` page(s). Be sure to begin your list of works cited with the words Works Cited centered in standard font (not underlined, not bolded, not italicized, and/or not in quotation marks).

Spacing

Double-space the entire text of the paper, from the heading (if you are not using a title page) to the last bibliographic entry in your list of works cited. For paragraphs, indent one-half inch (usually the first tab). For long (block) quotes (those which take up four or more lines of your paper), indent one inch (usually the second tab) for each line of the quotation.

MODEL PAPER

The following paper, "Taking Up the Cross: The Existential Jesus," by Holly A. Easttom, is a research paper in MLA style. The entire paper appears first in MLA style not requiring a title page. After the Works Cited are a title page, a formal outline (with lower case Roman numerals for page numbers), and the first page of the paper as it should look when a title page is used.

[The headers for this manuscript are missing so that the correct page numbers could be present for the entire manuscript. The computer disk has a correct version of this manuscript.]

Holly A. Easttom

Dr. Stephen Law

Early Christian Thought

29 November 1999

Taking Up the Cross: The Existential Jesus

The New Testament is the product of a marriage between Greek philosophy and early

Judaism. To best approach biblical understanding, then, it is necessary to adopt a universal vehicle:

one that addresses the question of human existence. For that reason, a theistic, existential approach

to scriptural understanding of the New Testament offers a strong foundation for interpretation.

This interpretation is supported by the fact that philosophy played a role in the formulation of

Christianity; but more importantly, it is supported by the actual teachings of Jesus.

The arrival of Alexander the Great introduced Hellenistic culture to the Near East. By the

time of early Christianity, the influence of Greek philosophy in the region was profound. Among

the schools of thought to influence Christianity was the Aristotelian concept of dualism, or the

discipline of body and emotions to allow reason to achieve the virtue of knowledge (Duling and

Perrin 66). This view employed contrasts of flesh/spirit, vice/virtue, and evil/good that greatly

influenced Gnostic Christians, Paul, and John the Baptist. Equally, as Honderich notes, the "Stoic

view of divinity and its relation to the world" as well as their concept of brotherhood were

historically influential in the development of Christian thought (853). The Cynics, or self-

proclaimed "citizens of the world," declared allegiance to no customs or class and lived by the

notion of "reducing wants to what can easily be achieved to take up their knapsack and follow

Heracles" (Honderich 174). This sense of detachment and wandering is later echoed by Christian

wanderers. According to Duling and Perrin, "There are some parallels between Cynic-Stoic

lifestyles and those of Jesus and the early apostles, most visible in austerity and apostolic mission.

Also the Cynic-Stoic literary style of arguing with an imaginary opponent and the habit of listing virtues and vices are characteristic devices of the apostle Paul" (68). The Cynics were also famous for using aphorisms and parables, which the synoptic gospels portray as Jesus's main mode of communication with the disciples. Early Christians also developed "schools" that were similar in structure to the philosophic schools of thought.

Not only did philosophy play a major role in the evolution of Christianity, it influenced the authors of the New Testament and more than likely influenced the subject of the text: Jesus. Born in the region of Galilee, Jesus was an intellectual who, according to Bidstrup,

> understood at least the rudiments of Greek philosophy and the complex
>
> theology of the Semitic Jews around him. We now know the teachings of
>
> Jesus paint the picture of a social iconoclast who, born into the volatile
>
> mixture of the cultural tensions of northern Palestine, saw the opportunity
>
> to pit a nearly secular Hellenized philosophy against the highly specific
>
> moralism of Judaism. (7)

With the establishment of philosophy within the Christian tradition, it is possible to interpret the New Testament with a theistic existential application. Existentialism, in a broad definition, is the notion that an individual achieves full potential by engaging the will to make choices and commitments that give a sense of practical identity that serves to fill his/her existence. As Honderich observes, "Sartre formulates the position as one in which the role of choice in human life is absolutely fundamental" (260). In summation, existentialism is the acknowledgement of absolute freedom and absolute responsibility for that freedom. It is the belief that every action implies a choice and that those choices determine an individual's essence, which must come to terms with absurdity. In short, it is not a philosophy for weaklings or cowards.

"Do not think that I came to bring peace on earth. I did not come to bring peace but a sword" (NKJV, Matt. 10:34) perfectly illustrates the idea that Jesus's message was not a rallying cry of peace but of opposition. Similarly, existentialism is not a social vision or utopia but one of the individual and how he/she faces his/her own existence. Instead of, as Shermer suggests, "giving a firm foundation for setting the conscience of man at rest forever" (78), this statement is perceived as a threat, or what Berryman terms a "mixture of the fear of responsibility and the fear of groundlessness in life" (31). This verse illustrates the combatant attitude man has toward his existence or, as Martin Buber phrased it, the refusal of the believing man to "remove himself from the concrete situation [of his existence], even if in the form of fighting against it" (312). A sword is that which separates or divides, and "Christ is a living sword," according to Sanford, "dividing and separating what was once merged together in order that individual differentiation may take place" (59).

This "battle cry" is the acceptance of responsibility that follows acknowledgement of absolute freedom. Man is responsible for accepting the consequences of his own actions and creating his own essence, as is clear in the following passage: "And he who does not take up his cross and follow Me is not worthy of Me. He who finds his life will lose it, and he who loses his life for My sake will find it" (Matt. 10:38-39). To realize one's full potential, one must take up his/her cross, or take responsibility for his/her actions and accordingly invest his/her life with meaning. To "lose his life for My sake" does not imply the loss of will or identity but the loss of the false self in return for the true, authentic self. It is the loss of social identity for the discovery of individual identity, or, as Jaspers notes, "to give up oneself to become oneself" (275). "If anyone desires to come after Me, let him deny himself, and take up his cross, and follow Me" (Matt. 16:24). This is not, as Sartre has said, the practice of "man losing himself as man so that God may be born" (246) but the realization of absolute freedom and removal of all constraints to, in

Heidegger's words, "sacrifice our human being for the preservation of the truth" (255). Later, Jesus says, "No one can come to Me unless the Father, who sent Me, draws him," and then, without coming to Jesus, "you have no life in you" (John 6:53). It is impossible to come to Jesus/salvation without first taking responsibility for personal choices and actions. Subsequently, without taking responsibility, there is no meaningful life.

In existential terms, this leads to either the embrace or avoidance of an absurd existence. It is here that one stands on the ridge before the leap, overwhelmed by both the incredible responsibility of creating his/her own essence and the meaningless prospect of inevitable death. Sartre refers to this initial reaction as "nausea," but *phobos* may be a more accurate term for this condition. *Phobos*, or fear of God, is that which, according to Buber, "comes when our existence between birth and death becomes incomprehensible and uncanny, when security is shattered through mystery and through this dark gate the believing man steps forth into the everyday which is henceforth hallowed as the place in which he has to live with the mystery" (312). According to Albert Camus, man has the following options: embrace absurdity or deny the absurdity by committing intellectual or physical suicide. In theistic terms, this equates to choosing between embracing the absurdity of mortality by accepting human limitations and following God or ignoring the incredible responsibility and committing intellectual suicide, thus, the "existential trade-off: embrace freedom and the resulting anxiety or surrender freedom to reduce the vertigo" (qtd. in Spohn 35). This choice is perhaps the most important of all.

To deny the responsibility of individual action is to deny freedom in an attempt to cast off the sense of isolation that accompanies absolute freedom. It is intellectual suicide, or what Haitch terms a state of "spiritual non-being which is manifested in emptiness and meaningless and is just as fundamental as the threat of physical death" (87). Ignoring the absurdity of mortality is to exist in what Heidegger calls "sheer timidity, [to] shut out our ears to the soundless voice which attunes us to the horror of the abyss" (258). There is no cure for existential anxiety; "there is only truth," according to Berryman, "but the truth can make us free when we accept our limits and discover the larger presence of God" (522). To discover truth, the absurdity of mortality must be embraced. The recognition of human limitations and acceptance of responsibility is what "you shall know as the truth, and the truth shall make you free" (John 8:32). This recognition leads to the development of conscious, thinking individuals responsible for their own actions as well as their own salvation; this salvation is what Haight calls "universally relevant for the whole of humankind, and in that sense Jesus is normatively true for the whole human race" (284). The truth is the recognition and acceptance of freedom. To ignore that freedom, to commit intellectual and spiritual suicide, is to remain in self-made bondage and to live and die a meaningless life. Taliaferro's observation that "the reality of death, the prophetic center of Christianity, is the critique of egoism; salvation is conceived of its overcoming" (3) then serves as a theistic existential interpretation of John 11:25: "He who believes in me, though he may die, he shall live." Faith, then, notes Taliaferro, "resides even under the shadow of dying" (4). To confront the absurdity is to live a meaningful life—to embrace Roffey's notion that "we are free to be anything but unfree" (131), and to commit oneself to that notion with passion: "Am I not an apostle? Am I not free?" (1 Cor. 9:1).

Embracing chaos in a Christian existential sense is a tool for grounding faith, because, according to Heidegger, "a faith that does not perpetually expose itself to the possibility of unfaith is no faith but merely a convenience" (255). M. R. Butz "defined chaos as a state of overwhelming anxiety and discussed the progression from chaos to a new form or a higher order of being as the transcendent cycle" (qtd. in Watts 92). Chaos in this context serves as tribulation to test faith in God. "Chaos, when encountered," notes Watts, "is to be embraced and fully experienced rather than eschewed and avoided. Chaos is not an evil to be avoided but rather an opportunity to be embraced. For example, Rom. 8:28-29 indicates that 'good' is not judged by what is pleasant or unpleasant but rather what is a catalyst for spiritual growth" (94). Chaos, therefore, is a part of a spiritual process toward maturation and wholeness, as is seen in John 17:33: "In the world you will have tribulation; but be of good cheer, I have overcome the world." The existential Jesus leads into unavoidable absurdities that must be overcome to become aware of Him. Through what Jaspers terms "our awareness of His being, this God can teach us to bear our own mortality, agony that in this world all I love, I myself must die, this agony is acknowledged and comprehended without delusion" (276).

To be free of delusion, one must embrace the mystery of life and divinity as an absurdity. As John 3:8 states, "The wind blows where it wishes, and you hear the sound of it, but cannot tell where it comes from and where it goes. So is everyone who is born of the spirit." There is the element of the unknown in the universe, and it is to be embraced. The emphasis is not on the unknown but on the controllable. While one cannot direct the universe, one can direct him- or herself, which is the message illustrated in John 8:14: "I know where I come from and where I am going, but you do not know where I come from and where I am going," which is why Jesus called the Kingdom a mystery. Thus, according to Sanford, "A mysterion was something to be known, but it was an initiated knowledge, knowledge that a person could acquire only through his or her individual insight or experience" (29).

Once the existential dilemma is acknowledged, there is no turning back: "No one, when he has lit a lamp, covers it with a vessel or puts it under a bed" (Luke 8:16). The same sentiment is expressed in Luke 11:33-35: "No one, when he has lit a lamp, puts it in a secret place or under a basket, but on a lampstand. [. . .] Therefore take heed that the light which is in you is not darkness." The acknowledgement of absurdity is not a source of darkness but a source of light, as John 12:35-36 illustrates: "Walk while you have the light, lest the darkness overtake you; he who walks in darkness does not know where he is going." After embracing the complexities of his/her

145

existence, one is bound to remain in that state of illumination; to do otherwise is cowardly. "But now after you have known God, or rather are known by God, how is it that you turn again to the weak and beggarly elements to which you desire again to be in bondage?" (Gal. 4:9). To ignore the existential responsibility is to willingly submit to slavery, which is an unnatural state for individuals, who are "not children of the bondwoman but of the free" (Gal. 4:31). Hence, there is no turning back because to do so would be to remove meaning and deny the authentic self. As Luke 9:62 states, "Jesus said, no one having put his hand to the plow, and looking back, is fit for the kingdom of God." In short, Jesus's message was not meant for cowards or for those afraid to act.

The taking up of one's "cross" is a deliberate choice and a conscious action; it is what Roffey calls "being-in-the-world as an active process" (137). According to Luke, "For everyone who asks receives, and he who seeks finds, and to him who knocks it will be opened" (11:10). Augustine equated God with truth, and the quest for truth is the quest for wisdom. It is, as Vaught terms it, "the act of will that enables us to reach beyond ourselves toward the ground of our existence" (324). Jesus himself said He was "the Way, the Truth, and the Life" (John 13:6), and to come to that truth is an intentional action that permeates human existence. Not to choose, not to act, and not to think are to deny life. Jesus spoke in parables because they engage the "right brain" of His listeners: individuals. "The kingdom of heaven is like a merchant seeking beautiful pearls" (Matt. 13:45) and equally involved. Jesus assumed the role of teacher because his message was meant to be attained via an ongoing learning process, designed to intrigue and stimulate. The message, as Bidstrup points out, is that "there is a kingdom of God, not of this world or the next, but one within you, and it is there you should look for your salvation" (7). Jesus instructed the disciples to "test all things; hold fast what is good" (1 Thess. 5:21). Paul Tillich claims, "people do not only ask questions, but they are the question they ask" (qtd. in Griffiss 218). Perhaps this is

146

also the purpose behind the "hard sayings" of Jesus; they were designed to be difficult to understand to engage critical thinking. For example, Jesus says in John 5:31, "If I bear witness of myself, my witness is not true." This reference may be to self-discovery or a truth resulting from individual thought and action. Existence is a logical, thinking discipleship, and this particular "hard saying" may well exemplify that notion.

"Whoever does not bear his cross and come after me cannot be my disciple" (Luke 14:27). To be a "disciple" involves continual decision-making and action; it is an ongoing process because each day presents new situations and doubts. To be authentic, according to Stackhouse, "we have to admit doubt and relativity into our consciousness—and then marshal the courage to be on the other side of doubt about being and worth" (100). Individuals need courage to embrace absurdity, chaos, and tribulation because they are essential to life. Without what Jones calls the occasional "abrasive brush with the unexpected, human life soon becomes a mere matter of routine; and before we know where we are, a casual indifference takes over and we die inside" (84). The untried life is empty, as is the untried self. Jesus himself said to God, "I do not pray you should take them out of the world, but that you should keep them from the evil one" (John 17:15). The "evil one' in this sense could be an individual's unrealized potential. Not only is an individual bound to "bear his own load" (Gal. 6:5) but also to fulfill his potential, as is expressed in the "Parable of Talents" in Matt. 25:14-30. A servant was given one talent and was unwilling to discover its potential. He "was afraid and went and hid the talent in the ground" (25:25). This "unprofitable" servant represents the undiscovered potential of every individual and was "cast into the outer darkness" (25:30) for his failure to act. Roffey observes, "Refusal to exercise the will to be oneself results in unrealized potential" (137) and detracts from a meaningful existence. One finds fulfillment, according to Sartre, by "seeking outside of himself a goal which is just this liberation, just this particular fulfillment" (244). Every individual is free to select the conditions that will best facilitate the realization and expression of his/her highest potential, and, observes Shermer, "The closer one comes to reaching the personal upper limit of potential, the greater the achievement" (86) and the greater the investment of meaning.

"Christianity," according to Spohn, "offers many powerful symbols that encourage the realization of human potential; the portrait of Christ provided by the Gospels offers an incredible example of authenticity—the term Christian means to be Christlike" (35). Perhaps this is what Christ meant when he said, "You are gods" (John 10:34); the freedom to choose and direct one's life gives humankind the power and responsibility of gods. "Man discovers himself when he discovers God," offers Vaught, "he discovers something that is identical with himself although it transcends him infinitely" (322). In John, Jesus told the disciples, "My father loves me, because I lay down my life that I may take it again. No one takes it from Me, but I lay it down of myself. I have power to lay it down, and I have power to take it again" (10:17). Individuals are similar to Jesus in that they have the power to "lay down" the false self in exchange for an authentic, meaningful self. In that sense, individuals are like a god.

The teachings attributed to Jesus make no excuses: "whatever a man sows, that he will also reap" (Gal. 6:7). The message of Jesus is one of startling liberation and responsibility. Just as Moses is the universal symbol for leadership and liberation in the Old Testament, Jesus is the symbol for liberation in the New Testament. Both make an unambiguous point: no slavery. Just as Moses led the Exodus from Egypt, Christ leads the Exodus out of ignorance by illuminating the freedom of will. It is a message of either damnation or salvation, dependant entirely upon the decision of the interpreter.

Shakespeare alleged that the Bible could be made to advocate anything anyone desired. Perhaps that was the purpose of the text—that it be a universal guide for living applicable to any interpretation. If true, then truth is the result of personal revelation, not uniform belief. Once an individual comes to his/her own personal reconciliation with the world, the Bible can be used as a foundation for knowledge and guidance. The interpretation of the text is ultimately the result of the reader's choices and use of will. The New Testament, then, is not just an accounting of the persecution and crucifixion of a prophet; it is the message of an existential Jesus.

Works Cited

Berryman, Jerome. "Teaching Presence and the Existential Curriculum." <u>Religious Education</u> 85 (1985): 509-35.

Bidstrup, Scott. "A Rational, Secular Perspective on the History of Christianity and its Scripture." <u>The Real Origins</u>. 24 May 1997. 13 Nov. 1999 <http://www.pe.net/~bidstrup/bible.htm>.

Buber, Martin. "Eclipse of God." Friedman 311-15.

Duling, Dennis C., and Norman Perrin, eds. <u>The New Testament: Proclamation and Parenesis, Myth and History</u>. 3rd ed. Fort Worth: Harcourt, 1994.

Friedman, Maurice, ed. <u>The Worlds of Existentialism: A Critical Reader</u>. Atlantic Highlands, NJ: Humanities, 1964.

Griffiss, James. "Thomas Aquinas, Paul Tillich, and the Anglican Theological Review." <u>Anglican Theological Review</u> 76 (1994): 212-25.

Haight, Roger. "The Case for Spirit Christology." <u>Theological Studies</u> 53 (1992): 257-87.

Haitch, Russell. "How Tillich and Kohut Both Find Courage in Faith." <u>Pastoral Psychology</u> Nov. 1995: 83-98.

Heidegger, Martin. "Introduction to Metaphysics." Friedman 254-66.

Honderich, Ted, ed. <u>The Oxford Companion to Philosophy</u>. New York: Oxford UP, 1995.

Jaspers, Karl. "Metaphysics." Friedman 274-82.

Jones, Alan. <u>Soulmaking: The Desert Way of Spirituality</u>. San Francisco: Harper, 1989.

The NKJV Greek English Interlinear New Testament. Trans. Arthur Farstad, et al.

    Nashville: Nelson, 1994.

Roffey, Arthur E. "Existentialism in a Post-Modern World: Meaningful Lessons for the

    Counselor." Counseling and Values 37 (1993): 129-48.

Sanford, John A. The Kingdom Within: The Inner Meaning of Jesus' Sayings. San

    Francisco: Harper, 1970.

Sartre, Jean-Paul. "The Flies." Friedman 246-49.

Shermer, Michael. "The Secular Sphinx: The Riddle of Ethics Without Religion." Skeptic

    4.2 (1996): 78-87.

Spohn, William C. Rev. of Biblical Interpretation and Christian Ethics, by J. I. H.

    McDonald. Theological Studies 55 (1994): 746-48.

Stackhouse, M. L. "What Tillich Meant to Me." Christian Century 107.4 (1990): 99-103.

Taliaferro, Charles. "Events of Grace: Naturalism, Existentialism, and Theology. A

    Review." The Review of Metaphysics 52 (1998): 449-50.

Vaught, Carl. "Faith and Philosophy." Monist 75 (1992): 325-26.

Watts, Richard. "Chaos and Christianity: A Response to Butz and a Biblical Alternative."

    Counseling and Values 41 (1997): 88-97.

Outline

<u>Thesis statement</u>: The New Testament is a product of a marriage between late Judaism and Greek philosophy; therefore, an existential interpretation of the New Testament is not only valid, it is supported by the text itself.

I. Introduction of philosophy to early Christianity

    A. Arrival of Alexander the Great

        1. Aristotelian concept of dualism and discipline of the flesh

        2. Gnostic influences on John the Baptist

        3. Stoicism and its concept of brotherhood

        4. Cynicism and the use of aphorisms as a literary tool

    5. Early Christian "schools" similar in structure to philosophical schools of thought

    B. Philosophical influences on writers of the New Testament and Jesus Christ

II. Existentialism as an interpretive tool for the New Testament

    A. Existentialism as the acknowledgement of absolute freedom

    B. Existentialism often viewed as a combatant relationship

    C. Creation of one's own essence

        1. Matthew 10:38-39

        2. Matthew 16:24 and "taking up the cross"

    D. Existentialism as a meaningful existence possible only through taking responsibility

        1. Sartre's reference to nausea

        2. New Testament references to <u>phobos</u>, or fear

    E. Albert Camus's choices in human existence

1. Intellectual suicide

2. Physical suicide

3. Recognition of absurd existence and construction of meaningful life

   a. John 8:32 and acceptance through truth

   b. Absurdity as a tool for meaningful growth toward authenticity

III. Existentialism in Christianity

A. Embracement of absurdity as liberation

B. The "hard sayings" of Jesus as a cerebral tool to engage philosophical thinking

C. Man as expected to fulfill his potential or reach authenticity in existentialist terms

   1. John 17:51, Galatians 6:5

   2. "Parable of Talents" and the importance of reaching individual potential

IV. Christian, Existential Authenticity

V. Conclusion

Taking Up the Cross: The Existential Jesus

The New Testament is the product of a marriage between Greek philosophy and early Judaism. To best approach biblical understanding, then, it is necessary to adopt a universal vehicle: one that addresses the question of human existence. For that reason, a theistic, existential approach to scriptural understanding of the New Testament offers a strong foundation for interpretation. This interpretation is supported by the fact that philosophy played a role in the formulation of Christianity; but more importantly, it is supported by the actual teachings of Jesus.

The arrival of Alexander the Great introduced Hellenistic culture to the Near East. By the time of early Christianity, the influence of Greek philosophy in the region was profound. Among the schools of thought to influence Christianity was the Aristotelian concept of dualism, or the discipline of body and emotions to allow reason to achieve the virtue of knowledge (Duling and Perrin 66). This view employed contrasts of flesh/spirit, vice/virtue, and evil/good that greatly influenced Gnostic Christians, Paul, and John the Baptist. Equally, as Honderich notes, the "Stoic view of divinity and its relation to the world" as well as their concept of brotherhood were historically influential in the development of Christian thought (853). The Cynics, or self-proclaimed "citizens of the world," declared allegiance to no customs or class and lived by the notion of "reducing wants to what can easily be achieved to take up their knapsack and follow Heracles" (Honderich 174). This sense of detachment and wandering is later echoed by Christian wanderers. According to Duling and Perrin, "There are some parallels between Cynic-Stoic lifestyles and those of Jesus and the early apostles, most visible in austerity and

Taking Up the Cross:

The Existential Jesus

by

Holly A. Easttom

Early Christian Thought

Dr. Stephen Law

29 November 1999

GRAMMAR

APOSTROPHES

There are two reasons to use apostrophes:

- to show possession

- to contract

POSSESSION

The English language is very regular about showing possession. In fact, English has no "exceptional" possessives. In other words, we use **'s** or **'** without fail.

- Use **'s** after a **singular noun:**

  John's boat   the player's fault   James's garden

  the dog's bowl   Mary's coat   her friend's brother

- Use **'** after a **plural noun:**

the cats' dishes (dishes belonging to more than one cat)

the Smiths' car (a car owned by more than one Smith)

the students' assignments (the assignments of the students)

- Use **'s** after irregular plurals:

the men's suits   the children's toys   the women's project

TRICKY POINTS:

- While the plural of **brother-in-law** is **brothers-in-law**, the possessive is **brother-in-law's**. The possessive plural is **brothers-in-law's**.

Names that end in –s:

- Mr. Thomas owns a home. That home is **Mr. Thomas's** home.
- Mr. And Mrs. Williams have a home. That home is the **Williamses'** home. (The tricky point here is that the proper noun needs to be made plural before the possessive is added. Thus, for instance, the plural of Jones is **Joneses**, and the plural of Douglass is **Douglasses**. To make them possessive, simply add ', as in the **Joneses'** vacation or the **Douglasses'** cabin.)

Another example:

You are addressing party invitations to the Weaver family and the Jones family. What do you write on the envelope?

- The **Weavers**
- The **Joneses**

Thus, you will be mailing the **Weavers'** invitation as well as the **Joneses'** invitation. Or you could say that you are mailing the **Weavers'** and the **Joneses'** invitations. If, however, someone named Weaver and someone named Jones share a residence and you are mailing only one invitation, then you are mailing the **Weaver and Jones's** invitation (to show possession of the same item by more than one person).

If Pat Jones and Chris Weaver host a party together, it's **Pat and Chris's party,** but if each one has a party, then it's **Pat's and Chris's parties.**

CONTRACTION

Use an apostrophe where you remove letters to show contraction:

do n<u>ot</u>	→ don't	Governmen	→ gov't
could <u>have</u>	→ could've (not could of!)	Continued	→ cont'd
he <u>will</u>	→ he'll	it <u>is</u>	→ it's*
can<u>not</u>	→ can't	who <u>is</u>	→ who's*

*<u>It's</u> is the contraction of <u>it is</u>. <u>Its</u> shows possession, like <u>my</u>, <u>your</u>, and <u>their</u>. <u>Who's</u> is the contraction of <u>who is</u> while <u>whose</u> is a possessive form (as in "Whose socks are on the floor?").

Apostrophes—Exercise 12

In the corresponding blanks below, add or delete apostrophes as necessary by writing the correct word. You may have to modify spelling by adding and/or deleting letters in some words. If the word is correct, write OK in the corresponding blank.

Recently, I inherited a pair of cats'[1] to go with the two kitten's[2] I already owned—or, I should say, who already owned me. Watching the four of them interact has brought great joy to my family, especially to my three daughter's[3]. One of the cat's[4] I inherited, Gracie, was also still a kitten when she came to live with us. The other, Gloria, is about to turn twelve, which figure's[5] up to about 84 in human year's[6]. Jake, the only boy in the group, seem's[7] to be the boss cat and has determined which dish is his'[8] and which dishes'[9] belong to the girls'[10]. To keep them all happy and to make our live's[11] easier, the cats'[12] dishes are kept together, along with bowl's[13] of water. Stella, our other original cat and the youngest of the four, spend's[14] a lot of time trying to upset Gloria because she believe's[15] that Gloria is "top cat." In truth, Gloria is perfectly happy being ignored by the rest of them except for occasional bath's[16] from Gracie. At first, the four of them did'nt[17] get along particularly well, but over time and with some coaxing from all of us, they interact well now that several months[18] have passed. Sometime's[19] I actually catch as many as three of them curled up together to nap during the day. At night, it's[20] another story when each of my daughters[21] want's[22] a cat to cuddle. Then there's[23] always the argument about who's[24] turn it was to clean the litter boxes'[25] because she who cleans the litter boxes that day has first choice as to which cat to cuddle that night.

1. _____   2. _____

3. _____   4. _____

5. _____   6. _____

7. _____   8. _____

9. _____   10. _____

11. _____   12. _____

13. _____   14. _____

15. _____   16. _____

17. _____   18. _____

19. _____   20. _____

21. _____   22. _____

23. _____   24. _____

25. _____

Apostrophes—Exercise 13

In the corresponding blanks below, add or delete apostrophes as necessary by writing the correct word. You may have to modify spelling by adding and/or deleting letters in some words. If the word is correct, write OK in the corresponding blank.

Two night's[1] ago, a pizza delivery driver stopped at our house to ask for direction's[2]. He was looking for two house's[3] he thought were on our street, but in reality, they were on the street behind our's[4]. Adding to his confusion was the fact that the name's[5] on both orders[6] read "Jones." We were sure that the pizza's[7] he was trying to deliver would be cold before much longer, so we tried to explain quickly that one family of Joneses'[8] lived directly behind us while the other Jones's[9] lived across the street from them. He did'nt[10] seem to understand what we were telling him. Then he explained that it was his first week delivering pizzas'[11] and that he kept getting lost driving through different neighborhood's[12] and trying to read house number's[13] in the dark. At one point, he said, all the pizza boxes'[14] he had piled in the car had fallen off the seat and landed sideway's[15] on the floor when he'd[16] slammed on his brake's[17] in front of one house. We tried not to laugh, but we could'nt[18] help ourselves'[19] because his story was so funny. He finally calmed down a bit, and we explained again about where the Joneses'[20] were on the next street. We still do'nt[21] know whether the Jones'[22] families'[23] ever got their pizza's[24] that night or whether the pizzas they got were their's[25] because we fully expected him to confuse the orders before he managed to deliver them.

1. _____ 2. _____

3. _____ 4. _____

5. _____ 6. _____

7. _____ 8. _____

9. _____ 10. _____

11. _____ 12. _____

13. _____ 14. _____

15. _____ 16. _____

17. _____ 18. _____

19. _____ 20. _____

21. _____ 22. _____

23. _____ 24. _____

25. _____

CAPITALIZATION

Capitalization is a part of English grammar that dictates the appropriate use of proper nouns and adjectives i.e., names, places, and things as well as the beginning of a new sentence. The examples will acquaint you with the do's and don'ts of capitalization using the APA format.

- Capitalize the first letter of the first word in a sentence.

  The sessions for the conferences are to be held inside.

- Capitalize the first letter after a colon if it is used to begin a subtitle in a literary citation.

  Student to student: A new form of communication (book title)

  Anderson, C. E. & Whittfield, J. (1999). Psychological terms : A new form of communication (1st ed.) . Boston: Allyn and Bacon. (book reference)

- Capitalize the first letter of the first word of a proper noun that is hyphenated.

  Ellen Cole-Thomas (proper noun)

- Capitalize other hyphenated words only when they begin a sentence.

  Mothers-in-law are helpful in acquiring family histories.

- Capitalize proper nouns and adjectives including proper names and derivatives of proper name, abbreviations of names, brand names, holidays, historical events, days of the week, months of the year, street names, cities and states, monuments, drug trade names, and geographical locations.

- Capitalize the first letter of titles of dignitaries, political offices, and ethnic groups, and religions when used in specific situations to designate specific individuals.

The President of the United States is Bill Clayton.

The Catholic Congress will meet in Kansas City, Mo.

The members of the new firm are Latinos.

Dean Edwards from the Department of Medicine at the University of California

will be the guest lecturer for new interns at the Blackburn Eye Clinic.

Capitalization—Exercise 14

Complete the following exercise using rules of capitalization. Circle any lower case letter(s) that should be capitalized in the paragraph. Place an X across any capitalized letter(s) that should be in lower case.

Strong bonds with Extended-family members have helped protect the development of many African-american children growing up in different environments with families often consisting of one parent. An opportunity for an extended family gathering would be kwanzaa. this is a cultural holiday celebrated between december 26 and january 1, by African -americans and African Descendants throughout the World. There are many other holidays celebrated by many Ethnic groups. A religious holiday celebrated by individuals of the jewish faith is Hanukkah. This holiday is also observed in december. Many corporations (such as general mills) provide funding for children during these the Winter season to prepare for the holidays. Celebrations for Employees are held in many areas of the u.s and also in Europe. Employers in most States only follow holiday observances that have been approved by the Governor and State Legislature.

COMMAS

Use commas to

- separate items in a list

- separate coordinate adjectives

- join independent clauses with a coordinate conjunction (*and, but, for, or, so, yet, nor*)

- set off introductory words, phrases, and clauses

- set off transitional elements and tag questions

- set off non-essential information

- separate quoted words from words of introduction or explanation

In addition, commas have specific uses in the addresses, dates, names, numbers, and correspondence.

ITEMS IN A LIST

The items can be individual words, phrases, or clauses, but they must be all the same type, or parallel in structure, and there need not always be a conjunction. (When the items in the list already contain commas, use semicolons to separate the items—see the section on semicolons.)

Words

→ red, white, and yellow   → ran, jumped, and slid

→ green, orange, blue   → sat, cried, sniffed

→ slowly, methodically, and deliberately   → dog, cat, and fish

→ quickly, easily, perfectly   → Pat, Terry, Chris

Phrases

→ Chris went to *the store, the library, and the pool.*

→ Marty took many items: *my book, her pencil, Pat's markers.*

→ I have looked *on the table, under the bed, and in the den.*

→ Pat believes in *thinking quickly, acting spontaneously, and enjoying completely.*

→ While you *watch television, chew gum, and fold laundry,* I will prepare dinner.

Clauses

→ Because *it's late, the weather is awful, and I am out of gas,* I'm staying home.

COORDINATE ADJECTIVES

Coordinate adjectives are those modifying words that carry equal weight when describing a noun.

To check whether to use a comma, add *and* between them or reverse the order. If either works, use

a comma between them.

→ *the happy little boy*	→ *two old books*
→ *the little happy boy* (yes)	→ *old two books* (no)
→ *the happy and little boy* (yes)	→ *two and old books* (no)
→ the happy, little boy (add comma)	→ two old books (no comma)

→ *the charming witty professor*	→ *many dear friends*
→ *the witty charming professor* (yes)	→ *dear many friends* (no)
→ *the charming and witty professor* (yes)	→ *many and dear friends* (no)
→ the charming, witty professor (add comma)	→ many dear friends (no comma)

INDEPENDENT CLAUSES

Use a comma before a coordinate conjunction (*and, but, for, or, so, yet, nor*) to join independent clauses (complete sentences). If one of the clauses is not independent, then do not use a comma with the conjunction.

Tom caught two fish. He ate one for dinner.

→ Tom caught two fish, and he ate one for dinner.

→ Tom caught two fish and ate one for dinner.

George was hungry. He ate Tom's other fish.

→ George was hungry, so he ate Tom's other fish.

The dog chased the ball. It rolled under the chair.

→ The dog chased the ball, and it rolled under the chair.

I am tired. I have work to finish.

→ I am tired, but I have work to finish.

→ I am tired but have work to finish.

She had a headache. She took a nap.

→ She had a headache, so she took a nap.

Jane did not like tonight's movie. She also didn't like the one we saw last week.

→ Jane did not like tonight's movie, nor did she like the one we saw last week.

→ Jane did not like tonight's movie nor the one we saw last week.

INTRODUCTORY WORDS, PHRASES, AND CLAUSES

Use a comma after introductory elements.

Words

→ *However,* he wanted a new gold fish.

→ *Consequently,* his parents bought him a fish.

→ *Tomorrow,* he will buy a second fish.

→ *Obviously,* he loves fish.

Phrases

→ *Early in the novel,* the author introduces the main characters.

→ *In the first chapter,* we meet Mitzi.

→ *Of all my cats,* Mutsy is my favorite.

→ *To let me know she's hungry,* she pushes her bowl to me.

→ *Sleeping on my feet,* Mutsy always knows when I awaken.

Clauses

→ *When the children went to school,* their parents celebrated.

→ *While the dog barked,* the rabbit ran away.

→ *Because ice covered the streets,* classes were cancelled.

→ *As I was telling you,* the store on the corner is having a sale.

→ *Although it is raining,* we will still have the picnic.

Commas: Items in a List—Exercise 15

Add commas where necessary to separate items in lists.

1. The children played with their toys puzzles and games.

2. Her brother mother sister and uncle sent cards for her birthday.

3. Johnny loved to sing dance and tap his foot to good music.

4. We had trouble starting the car checking into the hotel and finding our rooms.

5. We finally gave up had dinner and went home.

Commas: Coordinate Adjectives—Exercise 16

Add commas where necessary to separate coordinate adjectives.

1. The silly little kitten chased the brightly colored toy.

2. The very old tiger cat sharpened his long pointed claws on the old oak tree.

3. The carefree young girl sat on the old park bench.

4. My mother's oldest dearest friend bakes the best wheat bread.

5. Fred found a shiny new coin under the vending machine.

Commas: Independent Clauses—Exercise 17

Combine the following pairs of sentences using the coordinate conjunction in parentheses. Be sure to use a comma before the coordinate conjunction to join independent clauses. Rearrange and/or delete words where necessary.

1. The children splashed in the puddles. They got their pants wet. (*and*)

   _____

   _____

2. It continued to rain. The picnic was postponed. (*so*)

   _____

3. The students had not studied. They passed the quiz anyway. (*but*)

   _____

   _____

4. She gives her son cash for his birthday. She tells him not to spend it. (*yet*)

   _____

   _____

5. In her spare time, my aunt reads. She also knits. (*or*)

_____

_____

Commas: Introductory Words, Phrases, and Clauses—Exercise 18

Add commas where necessary to set off introductory words, phrases, and clauses.

1. At first we thought it was a big fish.

2. After a while we decided it wasn't an ordinary fish.

3. Finally we decided it was something very special.

4. Because it was so different we put it in a large fish tank.

5. In the morning we discovered it had doubled in size.

SEMICOLONS AND COLONS

Semicolons

There are two reasons to use **semicolons**:

1. to join closely related independent clauses

2. to separate items containing commas in a list

JOINING INDEPENDENT CLAUSES

Independent clauses (IC) are complete sentences. A comma does not have enough strength to join independent clauses without the help of a coordinate conjunction (<u>and</u>, <u>or</u>, <u>for</u>, <u>but</u>, <u>so</u>, <u>yet</u>, or <u>nor</u>), but a semicolon wields enough power to accomplish the task. Thus, on either side of a semicolon must be an independent clause: **IC; IC.**

Examples of joined sentences:

John studied many hours for the test. He had the highest score in the class.

→ John studied many hours for the test; he had the highest score in the class.

→ John studied many hours for the test, and he had the highest score in the class.

→ John studied many hours for the test and had the highest score in the class.

The rains came. The river overflowed its bank.

→ The rains came; the river overflowed its bank.

→ The rains came, and the river overflowed its bank.

→ When the rains came, the river overflowed its bank.

SEPARATING ITEMS IN A LIST

Occasionally, items in a list already contain commas, so it becomes confusing to separate those items with more commas. Semicolons replace the commas that would normally be used to separate the listed items.

Example:

The guest list included Jane Doe, the club president, Fred Smith, the vice president, Pat Jones, the treasurer, and Chris Wilson, the secretary.

While it is intuitively clear that only four people are actually listed, the punctuation identifies seven: (1) Jane Doe, (2) the club president, (3) Fred Smith, (4) the vice president, (5) Pat Jones, (6) the treasurer, and (7) Chris Wilson, the secretary. To cut the guest list almost in half, use semicolons:

The guest list included Jane Doe, club president; Fred Smith, vice president; Pat Jones, treasurer; and Chris Wilson, secretary.

Colons

Colons have some special uses including to separate hours and minutes (2:00 p.m.), to separate chapter and verse in Bible references (John 3:16), to separate titles from subtitles (*Working Wood: A Guide for the Country Carpenter*), and to conclude a salutation in a formal letter (Dear Dr. Whozit). But if a colon is used in a sentence outside its special uses, often to signal a forthcoming list or a restatement of the point made in the independent clause, it must be preceded by an independent clause: **IC:** _____.

Examples:

The guest list included the following people: Jane Doe, club president; Fred Smith, vice president; Pat Jones, treasurer; and Chris Wilson, secretary.

(Compare this example with the one above. In the previous sentence, "The guest list included" is not an independent clause, so there is no colon after included, but in this example, "The guest list included the following people" is a complete sentence and thus requires a colon before the list.)

The child stayed awake all night waiting for one person: Santa Claus.

(Compare with "The child stayed awake all night waiting for Santa Claus.")

Her backpack contained all the essential items: books, pencils, and scantrons.

(Compare with "Her backpack contained books, pencils, and scantrons.")

Moby-Dick begins with the following words: "Call me Ishmael."

(Compare with "*Moby-Dick* begins with 'Call me Ishmael'.")

Semicolons and Colons—Exercise 19

In the blanks below, add a semicolon (;) or colon (:) as needed. If no change is needed, add nothing to the blank.

Dear Mr. Smith__

Thank you for__ the games and books you sent to the children at__ the elementary school. They are looking forward to__ playing the games and reading the books, especially *Letters From Felix__ A Little Rabbit on a World Tour*. We truly appreciate your kindness and generosity__ we want you to know how much your gift means to__ the children and to us. If it is convenient for you, please join us at__ Homer Jones Elementary on__ Wednesday at 2__30 p.m. for a celebration of your gifts.

With kind regards,

Betsy Boss__ and Catherine Gump

Combine the following pairs of sentences using semicolons, colons, and/or conjunctions (with commas where required).

1. The cats ran across the room. They knocked over two potted plants.

   _____

   _____

   _____

2. Fred worked hard on his garden. It produced vegetables all summer.

   _____

   _____

3. Mary and her friends spent the day at the mall. They didn't buy anything.

   _____

   _____

   _____

4. The dog chased a butterfly. He never caught it.

   _____

   _____

   _____

5. We sent letters to several people. The letters went to the Smiths, the Joneses, and the Greens.

   _____

   _____

Semicolons, Colons, and Commas—Exercise 21

In the corresponding blanks below, add a comma, semicolon, or colon as needed. If no change is needed, add nothing to the blank.

Have you ever wondered how instant coffee is made? First (1)__ the coffee beans are prepared as they would be for regular coffee (2)__ they are roasted (3)__ blended (4)__ and ground. At the factory (5)__ workers brew great batches of coffee(6)__ 1800 to 2000 pounds (7) at a time. The coffee is (8)__ then (9)__ passed through tubes (10)__ under great pressure (11) at a high temperature. This process causes (12)__ much of the water to boil away (13) creating coffee liquor (14)__ with a high percentage of solids. At this point (15)__ a decision must be made about what the final product will be (16)__ powdered instant coffee (17)__ or freeze dried coffee. Powdered instant coffee is made by (18)__ heating the coffee liquor to 500 degrees F in a large dryer (19)__ which boils away the remaining water (20)__ the powdered coffee is simply gathered (21)__ from the bottom of the dryer (22)__ and packed. If freeze dried coffee is being made (23)__ the coffee liquor is frozen (24)__ into pieces (25)__ which are then broken into small granules. The granules are placed in (26)__ a vacuum box (27)__ a box containing no air (28)__ which turns the frozen water into steam (29)__ which is removed (30) all that is left are (31)__ coffee solids. Some people say (32)__ they prefer freeze (33)__ dried coffee (34)__ because (35)__ the high temperature (36)__ used to make regular instant coffee (37)__ destroys some of the flavor. Either way (38)__ the coffee is more convenient than (39) coffee (40)__ which is brewed at home.

VERBS

All actions take place in the past, the present, or the future and verbs are the words that express the action within a sentence; they change their form to accommodate tense and number. Most verbs typically change from present to past tense by ending the verb in ed or *s*. Many words require helping verbs to clarify action, for instance, forms of <u>to be</u> and <u>to have</u> help the main verbs in sentences. (When writing in APA Format always use the active voice).

Example

She jumps on the bed. *(present)*

I jumped on the bed to play with the dog. *(past)*

Andraya will jump on the bed when the dog barks. *(future)*

HELPING VERBS

Helping verbs are used to change verb tense. Some helping verbs are forms of <u>to be</u> and <u>to have</u> as well as should, could, would, may, might, and must.

IRREGULAR VERBS

These verbs change their spelling when used in the past tense, and helpers are needed to express the correct meaning within a sentence (Blumenthal, & Zahner, 1966).

Irregular verbs to name a few:

Present	Past	Past with Helpers
Begin	Began	have begun
Break	Broke	have broken
Choose	Chose	have chosen
Drive	Drove	have driven
Eat	Ate	have eaten
Fall	Fallen	have fallen
Grow	Grew	have grown
Know	Knew	have known
Leave	Left	have left
Lie	Lay	have lain
Lay	Laid	have laid
Sit	Sat	have sat
Speak	Spoke	have spoken
Take	Took	have taken
Throw	Threw	have thrown
Write	Wrote	have written

AGREEMENT EXTRAS

- Singular subjects are used with singular forms of verbs, as well as plural subjects are used with plural forms of verbs.

- The verb *to be* is the exception.

- The pronoun *you* is always considered plural.

- The simple past form of an irregular verb should never be used with a helper.

- The past form of a verb with a helper needs a helper to be considered as a verb.

- A verb must agree with its subject, not with a noun or pronoun that comes between the subject and the verb.

Verbs—Exercise 22

In the following paragraph there are numbers included in each sentence. Make the corrections by writing in the correct form of the verb and/or helping verbs. The lines provided at the end of the exercise correspond with the numbers in the sentence. Make your corrections on the lines and write correct when no correction is needed.

Dear Floyd,

(1)I would have wrote you before this, (2) but I have fallen into the age-old habit of putting things off until later. (3) I believe that I become lacks in fulfilling these tasks. (4) I went to visit Helen for my vacation. (5) I had never went on an airplane before. (6) The flight attendant assured us that everything would be fine. (7) The pilot must have broke every speed record to get us to our destination on time. (8) During the flight, I done the work on my book that have to be done by next month. (9) I stopped working long enough to see the movie.

(10) I left my seat and missed the snack. (11) When I returned, the other passengers was completing their sandwiches. (12) I begun to feel hungry. (13)Fortunately, I come back just in time for a beverage. (14) Shortly after the food service, it was time to prepare for landing. (15) This flight was the first time I took an airplane and I sit in my seat with the belt fastened during most of the time I was in the air. (16) The trip of course were a success. (17) I has a wonderful time also on my vacation to Texas. (18) From now on, when I find an inexpensive trip by airplane, I jumped at the opportunity to take it. (19) I will write again soon. (20) You can call me anytime and leave your number on the voice mail after my recorded message ends.

1. _____

2. _____

3. _____

4. _____

5. _____

6. _____

7. _____

8. _____

9. _____

10. _____

11. _____

12. _____

13. _____

14. _____

15. _____

16. _____

17. _____

18. _____

19. _____

20. _____

CORRECTED EXERCISES

RUNNING HEAD AND HEADER— CORRECTED EXERCISE 1

(answers may vary)

1.

                                                  Stress and Interpersonal Support   1

Running Head: STRESS AND INTERPERSONAL SUPPORT AMONG STUDENTS

2.

                                                        Conceptual Judgment   1

Running Head: ABSTRACT ORDER SCHEMA IN CONCEPTUAL JUDGEMENT

3.

                                        Personality Development in Adolescence   1

Running Head: INFLUENCE OF GENDER ON PERSONALITY DEVELOPMENT

4.

                                                  Conditioned Patellar Reflex   1

Running Head: STUDY OF THE CONDITIONED PATELLAR REFLEX

5.

                                          Judgment of Employment Potential   1

Running Head: DISABLITIES AND JUDGEMENT OF EMPLOYMENT POTENTIAL

6.

                                                  Sexual Selection Among House Crickets   1

Running Head: DOMINANCE RANKING AND SEXUAL SELECTION IN CRICKETS

7.

                                                  Gestalt Therapy and Eating Disorders   1

Running Head: GESTALT THERAPY WITH FEMALE ANOREXICS AND BULIMICS

8.

                                                  Effects of Caffeine on Nervous System   1

Running Head: EFFECTS OF CAFFEINE ON CENTRAL NERVOUS SYSTEM

9.

                                                  Mate Acquisition Among the Elderly   1

Running Head: AN EVOLUTIONARY APPROACH TO MATE ACQUISITION

10.

                                                  Review   1

Running Head: REVIEW OF "MAN'S SEARCH FOR MEANING"

ABBREVIATIONS—CORRECTED EXERCISE 2

1. IQ
2. REM
3. AIDS
4. STM
5. MMPI
6. e.g.,
7. etc.
8. i.e.,
9. viz.,
10. vs.
11. et al.,
12. cm
13. s, min, hr (s)
14. lb.
15. °
16. cps
17. dB
18. °C
19. deg/s
20. °F
21. g
22. in.
23. km
24. kg
25. kph
26. L
27. m
28. mg
29. meV
30. ml
31. mg
32. mm
33. mph
34. N
35. psi
36. rpm
37. V
38. W
39. kHz
40. vol.
41. wt.
42. g,
43. Hz

QUOTATIONS—CORRECTED EXERCISE 3

The issues of aging and retirement ate growing increasingly important in the United States. Advances in medicine and nutrition have increased longevity in our society and have prompted increased focus on the developmental life cycle of maturing individuals. Flowers indicated "the population would increase to thirty-four million by 2000". (Flowers, 1989) The "baby boomers" will increase the senior population by 2010 and they will make up the largest component of the U.S. population. Flower (1990) further stated that, "the 'baby boomer' will be the wealthiest group of seniors in U.S. history", page 4. Other demographers agree with Flowers and they believe that her estimate may be a bit conservative. Only time will tell the actual impact of this population boom.

Anders (1990) has speculated as to the changes that we can expect:

As a result of this increase of older adults in the mainstream of society, it is becoming increasingly more important that theorist and researchers understand many of the complex psychological and social issues relative to this expanding group of our society. Among other things, 'retirees' are likely to feel stress and anxiety in dealing with the role transitions, the prospect of isolation and loneliness, the possible loss of societal role and status, financial instability, and the inevitable decline in health and loss of independence.(p.4).

Anders (1991) "introduces the issue of the retirement role that the boomer will assume. Retirement became a tangible life event in 1935 with the enactment of Social Security legislation. The law provided individuals with a financial supplement in old age and thus established retirement as a social institution" (p.7).

Bowen, R. (1954, March). The joy of writing. *People*. 47-49.

Toby, E., Maxwell, C. & Carpenter, Q. (2000). A guide to marriage. *Family Issues,30*, 401-413.

Butler, W., Cooper, J., Bold, R. & White, B. (1996). *The tie that binds: A new edition.* New York: Bacon Publishers.

Mason, T. (1887). Returning to the south. In K. Wright & B. Wright (Eds.). *Insight on the cities in the south.* (pp. 104-109). Kansas City: McGraw- Hill.

Boss. A. Y. (1997). An examination of adult behavior: When stress is controlled (Doctoral dissertation, University of Maryland, 1997). *Dissertation Abstracts International, 31,* W80176.

Wilson, C. (1995). Spanish as a second language. Unpublished master's thesis, University of Texas, Austin.

Zane. G. E. & Falcon, B. (1988). The development of a politician [Review of the book *Politicians and Why*]. Los Angeles: Fox Publishers.

Eaton, W., Scott, R., Clarke, U. & Lyons, O. (1978). A new approach to teaching using technology. *Technology Today, 9,* 90-97.

Green, V., & Ball, K.(1991). Understanding behavior 101. *Psychology In the Twenty-First Century, 8,* 312-324.

Stanley, T. Y., Ross, E., Franklin, D. A. & Boyd, G. H. (in press). Relationships: A new beginning. *Directions.*

Hightower, Y. & Cobb, M. (1978). *Senior adulthood in different cultures.* Philadelphia: Macmillan.

Timberland, S. (1967). Life began at 40. In M. Hart (Ed.), *Developmental Issues for men and women.* (pp. 1234-1240). Kansas City: Dell.

Baxter, R., Young, L. & Grayson, O.P, (1988, January). Family histories using color genograms. Paper session presented at the biannual meeting of the American Society of Medicine, Alexander, SC.

Jordan, Z., (1989). The approach to examining child in dysfunctional families. Unpublished manuscript.

Simpson, W. (1998). The code of silence in Greek lettered organizations. [Review of film]. *Student service series, 6.*

REFERENCING—CORRECTED EXERCISE 6

Biggs, C., Hines, S., & Boost, D. (1978, May 5). Carl's private pain and confession. *Modern Maturity, 32,* 102 – 110.

Grouper, T., Bradley, T., Griggs, B., & Holmes, P. (1987). Schools and the new wave of technology. *Life in the Twenty First Century, 67,* 34-45.

Eden, R. (1990). *Computers made easy.* Boston: Allyn & Bacon.

Kane, K. E. (Ed.). (1967). *If ears could talk and eyes could hear.* Dallas, TX: Conan & Bass

Bronze, T. (1990). *Time, space, and the reality of life* (Rev. ed.). New York: Tisane Publishers.

Gains, J., Lake, W. A., & Shorts, P. (Eds.). (1991). *What is reality.* San Francisco: Cohn Publishers.

Smith, V., Jones, M., & Benton, L. (1981, May). *The art of volunteering.* Poster session presented at the third annual Meeting of Market Research, Denver, CO.

Wadley, L., & Edwards, W. L. (1976). An analysis of marital longevity. *Proceedings of the National Association for Families, 11,* 1186 – 1192.

Angel, C., & Edwards, V. (2000). [Review of the film Life begins at mid-life]. *Total Development, 5.*

Edwards, W. (1971). Life satisfaction and retirement. *Dissertation Abstract International , 54.* (UMI No. P50102)

Conn, H., Conn, H. M., & Conn, B. (1991). Rivalry among siblings: The influence of having twin sisters. *Journal of Child Psychology, 11,* 35 – 48.

Schmidt, I., & Cranem, Z. (1981). In search pf ethnic heritage. In B. Rogers & G. Stewart (Eds.), *American Heritage* (pp. 111-120). New York City: Marks.

WORKS CITED: BOOKS WITH 1-3 AUTHORS—CORRECTED EXERCISE 7

Works Cited

Barnet, Sylvan, Morton Berman, and William Burto. A
Dictionary of Literary Terms. Boston: Little, 1960.

Herriot, James. The Lord God Made Them All. New York: St.
Martin's, 1981.

Kinneavy, James L. A Theory of Discourse: The Aims of
Discourse. New York: Norton, 1980.

Ruland, Richard, and Malcolm Bradbury. From Puritanism to
Postmodernism: A History of American Literature. New
York: Viking, 1991.

Vonnegut, Kurt. Jailbird. New York: Dell, 1979.

---. Slapstick. New York: Dell, 1976.

WORKS CITED LIST— WORKS IN EDITED BOOKS—

CORRECTED EXERCISE 8

Works Cited

Auden, W. H. Introduction. Poe: Selected Prose and Poetry. Ed. Auden. Rev. ed. New York: Holt, 1964. v-xvii.

Maimon, Elaine P. Foreword. Writing in the Academic Disciplines, 1870-1990: A Curricular History. By David R. Russell. Carbondale: Southern Illinois UP, 1991. ix-xi.

Melville, Herman. "Monody." The Portable Melville. Ed. Jay Leyda. New York: Penguin, 1952. 593-94.

Thomas, Dylan. "And Death Shall Have No Dominion." The Collected Poems of Dylan Thomas. New York: New Directions, 1953. 77.

Weaver, Richard. "Language is Sermonic." The Rhetorical Tradition: Readings from Classical Times to the Present. Ed. Patricia Bizzell and Bruce Herzberg. Boston: Bedford, 1990. 1044-54.

WORKS CITED: NEWSPAPER AND MAGAZINE: ARTICLES, LETTERS TO THE EDITOR, EDITORIALS, AND REVIEWS— CORRECTED EXERCISE 9

Works Cited

Barker, Juliet. "A Year in the Life: A Microhistory of an Extraordinary Literary Collaboration." Rev. of The Gang: Coleridge, the Hutchinsons and the Wordsworths in 1802, by John Worthen. Atlantic Monthly Apr. 2001: 96-98.

Chastain, Jim, II. "Jolie Gives Indiana Jones Run for his Money." Rev. of Lara Croft: Tomb Raider, dir. Simon West. Edmond Sun [Edmond, OK] 17 June 2001: 13A.

Grey, Bernadette. "That Age-Old Question." Editorial. Working Woman Oct. 2000: 4.

Kirk, Don. "Seoul Nudges North Toward New Talks." New York Times 17 June 2001, natl. ed.: 10.

McCormick, John, and Steve Rhodes. "A Murderer Times Four: DNA Clues can Make Life Easier for Cops—or Tougher." Newsweek 6 Sept. 1999: 33.

Reiter, Ed. "2001 Coin Forecast: Numismatic Experts Look at the Year Ahead." Coinage Jan. 2001: 10+.

Walsh, Brendan. Letter. Atlantic Monthly Feb. 2001: 16.

WORKS CITED: JOURNALS—CORRECTED EXERCISE 10

Works Cited

"Annual Report Competition." Financial World 161.22 (1992): 70-80.Berlin, James A. "Poststructuralism, Cultural Studies, and the Composition Classroom: Postmodern Theory in Practice." Rhetoric Review 11 (1992): 16-33.

Kostelnick, Charles. "From Pen to Print: The New Visual Landscape of Professional Communication." Journal of Business and Technical Communication 8 (1994): 91-117.

"Typographical Design, Modernist Aesthetics, and Professional Communication." Journal of Business and Technical Communication 4 (1990): 5-24.

Miller, Carolyn. "Technology as a Form of Consciousness: A Study of Contemporary Ethos." Central States Speech Journal 29 (1978): 228-36.

Wiesendanger, Betsy. "Ben and Jerry Scoop Up Credibility." Public Relations Journal 38.8 (1993): 20.

Works Cited

The Beowulf Project. Ed. Donald Becker and Phil Merkey. 27

Apr. 2001. Scyld Computing. 21 May 2001 <http://

www.beowulf.org/>.

Mendell, David. "City Agency Defends Public Arts Spending:

Cultural Affairs Books Juggled." Chicago Tribune 9

June 2001. 9 June 2001 <http://www.chicagotribune.com/

news/metro/chicago/article/0,2669,ART-52336,FF.html>.

The Orlando Project: An Integrated History of Women's

Writing in the British Isles. Ed. Paul Dyck and Cathy

Grant. 2 May 2001. U of Alberta. 9 June 2001

<http://www.ualberta.ca/ORLANDO/>.

Schmidt, Ralph. Email to author. 22 Feb. 2001.

Showalter, Max. "Man Who Saved Old Tree Given Tree

Preservation Award." Journal and Courier Online

(Lafayette, IN) 25 May 2001. 3 June 2001

<http://www.lafayettejc.com/news0525/0525107.shtml>. Voyager

Project Home Page. May 2001. NASA. 4 June 2001

<http://vraptor.jpl.nasa.gov/voyager/voyager.html>.

APOSTROPHES—CORRECTED EXERCISE 12

Recently, I inherited a pair of <u>cats</u>[1] to go with the two <u>kittens</u>[2] I already owned—or, I should say, who already owned me. Watching the four of them interact has brought great joy to my family, especially to my three <u>daughters</u>[3]. One of the <u>cats</u>[4] I inherited, Gracie, was also still a kitten when she came to live with us. The other, Gloria, is about to turn twelve, which <u>figures</u>[5] up to about 84 in human <u>years</u>[6]. Jake, the only boy in the group, <u>seems</u>[7] to be the boss cat and has determined which dish is <u>his</u>[8] and which <u>dishes</u>[9] belong to the <u>girls</u>[10]. To keep them all happy and to make our <u>lives</u>[11] easier, the <u>cats'</u>[12] dishes are kept together, along with <u>bowls</u>[13] of water. Stella, our other original cat and the youngest of the four, <u>spends</u>[14] a lot of time trying to upset Gloria because she <u>believes</u>[15] that Gloria is "top cat." In truth, Gloria is perfectly happy being ignored by the rest of them except for occasional <u>baths</u>[16] from Gracie. At first, the four of them <u>didn't</u>[17] get along particularly well, but over time and with some coaxing from all of us, they interact well now that several <u>months</u>[18] have passed. <u>Sometimes</u>[19] I actually catch as many as three of them curled up together to nap during the day. At night, <u>it's</u>[20] another story when each of my <u>daughters</u>[21] <u>wants</u>[22] a cat to cuddle. Then <u>there's</u>[23] always the argument about <u>whose</u>[24] turn it was to clean the litter <u>boxes</u>[25] because she who cleans the litter boxes that day has first choice as to which cat to cuddle that night.

APOSTROPHES—CORRECTED EXERCISE 13

Two nights[1] ago, a pizza delivery driver stopped at our house to ask for directions[2]. He was looking for two houses[3] he thought were on our street, but in reality, they were on the street behind ours[4]. Adding to his confusion was the fact that the names[5] on both orders[6] read "Jones." We were sure that the pizzas[7] he was trying to deliver would be cold before much longer, so we tried to explain quickly that one family of Joneses[8] lived directly behind us while the other Joneses[9] lived across the street from them. He didn't[10] seem to understand what we were telling him. Then he explained that it was his first week delivering pizzas[11] and that he kept getting lost driving through different neighborhoods[12] and trying to read house numbers[13] in the dark. At one point, he said, all the pizza boxes[14] he had piled in the car had fallen off the seat and landed sideways[15] on the floor when he'd[16] slammed on his brakes[17] in front of one house. We tried not to laugh, but we couldn't[18] help ourselves[19] because his story was so funny. He finally calmed down a bit, and we explained again about where the Joneses[20] were on the next street. We still don't[21] know whether the Jones[22] families[23] ever got their pizzas[24] that night or whether the pizzas they got were theirs[25] because we fully expected him to confuse the orders before he managed to deliver them.

CAPITALIZATION—CORRECTED EXERCISE 14

Strong bonds with extended-family members have helped protect the development of many African-American children growing up in different environments with families often consisting of one parent. An opportunity for an extended family gathering would be Kwanzaa. This is a cultural holiday celebrated between December 26 and January 1, by African-Americans and African descendants throughout the world. There are many other holidays celebrated by many ethnic groups. A religious holiday celebrated by individuals of the Jewish faith is Hanukkah. This holiday is also observed in December. Many corporations (such as General Mills) provide funding for children during the winter season to prepare for various holidays. Celebrations for employees are held in many areas of the U.S. and also in Europe. Employers in most states only follow holiday observances that have been approved by the governor and state legislator.

(1) The children played with their toys, puzzles, and games.

(2) Her brother, mother, sister, and uncle sent cards for her birthday.

(3) Johnny loved to sing, dance, and tap his foot to good music.

(4) We had trouble starting the car, checking into the hotel, and finding our rooms.

(5) We finally gave up, had dinner, and went home.

COMMAS: COORDINATE ADJECTIVES—CORRECTED EXERCISE 16

(1) The silly, little kitten chased the brightly colored toy.

(2) The very old tiger cat sharpened his long, pointed claws on the old oak tree.

(3) The carefree, young girl sat on the old park bench.

(4) My mother's oldest, dearest friend bakes the best wheat bread.

(5) Fred found a shiny, new coin under the vending machine.

COMMAS: INDEPENDENT CLAUSES—CORRECTED EXERCISE 17

(answers may vary)

(1) *The children splashed in the puddles. They got their pants wet. (and)*

(a) The children splashed in the puddles**, and** they got their pants wet.

(b) The children splashed in the puddles **and** got their pants wet.

(2) *It continued to rain. The picnic was postponed. (so)*

(a) It continued to rain**, so** the picnic was postponed.

(3) *The students had not studied. They passed the quiz anyway. (but)*

(a) The students had not studied**, but** they passed the quiz anyway.

(b) The students had not studied **but** passed the quiz anyway.

(4) *She gives her son cash for his birthday. She tells him not to spend it. (yet)*

(a) She gives her son cash for his birthday**, yet** she tells him not to spend it.

(b) She gives her son cash for his birthday **yet** tells him not to spend it.

(5) *In her spare time, my aunt reads. She also knits. (or)*

(a) In her spare time, my aunt reads**, or** she knits.

(b) In her spare time, my aunt reads **or** knits.

COMMAS: INTRODUCTORY WORDS, PHRASES, AND CLAUSES—CORRECTED

EXERCISE 18

(1) At first, we thought it was a big fish.

(2) After a while, we decided it wasn't an ordinary fish.

(3) Finally, we decided it was something very special.

(4) Because it was so different, we put it in a large fish tank.

(5) In the morning, we discovered it had doubled in size.

Dear Mr. Smith:

Thank you for the games and books you sent to the children at the elementary school. They are looking forward to playing the games and reading the books, especially *Letters From Felix: A Little Rabbit on a World Tour*. We truly appreciate your kindness and generosity; we want you to know how much your gift means to the children and to us. If it is convenient for you, please join us at Homer Jones Elementary on Wednesday at 2:30 p.m. for a celebration of your gifts.

With kind regards,

Betsy Boss and Catherine Gump

SEMICOLONS AND COLONS—CORRECTED EXERCISE 20

(answers may vary)

(1) *The cats ran across the room. They knocked over two potted plants.*

(a) The cats ran across the room**;** they knocked over two potted plants.

(b) The cats ran across the room**, and** they knocked over two potted plants.

(c) The cats ran across the room **and** knocked over two potted plants.

(2) *Fred worked hard on his garden. It produced vegetables all summer.*

(a) Fred worked hard on his garden**;** it produced vegetables all summer.

(b) Fred worked hard on his garden**, and** it produced vegetables all summer.

(3) *Mary and her friends spent the day at the mall. They didn't buy anything.*

(a) Mary and her friends spent the day at the mall**;** they didn't buy anything.

(b) Mary and her friends spent the day at the mall**, and** they didn't buy anything.

(c) Mary and her friends spent the day at the mall **and** didn't buy anything.

(4) *The dog chased a butterfly. He never caught it.*

(a) The dog chased a butterfly**;** he never caught it.

(b) The dog chased a butterfly**, but** he never caught it.

(c) The dog chased a butterfly **but** never caught it.

(5) *We sent letters to several people. The letters went to the Smiths, the Joneses, and the Greens.*

(a) We sent letters to several people**:** the Smiths, the Joneses, and the Greens.

(b) We sent letters **to the** Smiths, the Joneses, and the Greens.

Have you ever wondered how instant coffee is made? First, the coffee beans are prepared as they would be for regular coffee: they are roasted, blended, and ground. At the factory, workers brew great batches of coffee: 1800 to 2000 pounds at a time. The coffee is then passed through tubes, under great pressure, at a high temperature. This process causes much of the water to boil away, creating coffee liquor with a high percentage of solids. At this point, a decision must be made about what the final product will be: powdered instant coffee or freeze dried coffee. Powdered instant coffee is made by heating the coffee liquor to 500 degrees F in a large dryer, which boils away the remaining water; the powdered coffee is simply gathered from the bottom of the dryer and packed. If freeze dried coffee is being made, the coffee liquor is frozen into pieces, which are then broken into small granules. The granules are placed in a vacuum box, a box containing no air, which turns the frozen water into steam, which is removed; all that is left are coffee solids. Some people say they prefer freeze dried coffee because the high temperature used to make regular instant coffee destroys some of the flavor. Either way, the coffee is more convenient than coffee which is brewed at home.

VERBS—EXERCISE 22

1. have written

2. correct

3. have become

4. correct

5. gone (or flown)

6. correct

7. have broken

8. did, has to be done

9. correct

10. correct

11. were

12. began

13. came

14. correct

15. sat

16. was

17. had

18. jump

19. correct

Bibliography

American Psychological Association. (2001). *Publication Manual of the American Psychological Association.* (5th ed.). Washington, D.C.: Author.

American Psychological Association. (1994). *Publication Manual of the American Psychological Association.* (4th ed.). Washington, D.C.: Author.

Blumenthal, J. C., Zahner, L., Frank, R. & Lazarus, A. (1966). *The English Language.* New York: Harcourt, Brace.

Gibaldi, Joseph. *MLA Handbook for Writers of Research Papers.* 5th ed. New York: MLA, 1999.

Hodges, J. C., & Whitten, M. E. (1967). *Harbrace College Handbook.* New York: Harcourt, Brace.

Teall, K.M. (1971). *Black history in Oklahoma: A resource book.* Oklahoma City: Oklahoma City Public School Title III, ESEA.